RUNNING WITH A PACK OF WOLVES

GILLY SHAW

HEAD-HUNTER BOOKS

First published in June 2005 by Head-Hunter Books
Reprinted 2005

ISBN 0-9548542-1-7

Head-Hunter Books

Printed in Great Britain
by MPG Books Limited, Bodmin

CONTENTS

ACKNOWLEDGMENTS

Firstly, I would like to thank the BBC for making me look the biggest clown ever to be seen on TV and to the Brummie twat who the BBC employed who said he knew me. Well Mr. BBC man, now everyone in the world can read about me. Anyway, f-ck them. This book is dedicated to a friend of mine who I respected in so many ways and for so many reasons, Mr. Dave Powers (FINGLES), who suddenly passed away and left his family, friends and his beloved Wolves. R.I.P. mate.

And to say thanks to all the lads i.e.

Joey, Chinny, Howey, Bona, Kings, Tyson, Shaun Spearsy, Colley, Nosha, the Kelly brothers, One Eye Milner, Dm, Norm, Chris and Rich, Carlton, Preston, Slater brothers, Painton, Abbos, all three of them, Spats, Lawley, Brummie Nick and Rob, the Telford lads, Grundy, Dancer, Laney, Fuzz….! Harding, Ben, Bungalow Ben, Adamsy, Faza, Puna, Jeff, Grandad, my mate, Dimebar, who never leaves me, Gaz and Steve Lees, Eddy, Monk, Dunham, Sarbo, plus my mates from other clubs, Daz, Christion, Ammy, Rich and Manley from Plymouth, Tony from Leicester, Bracken from Arsenal, Mr. Gypsy Pearly King, Jay Marraner and Fat Pat, both of Chelsea … also the Wolves Youth, the Twins, etc. Well lads, thanks for the best days of my life. If it weren't for you I wouldn't be writing this now … Cheers …

But most of all, this is for my Mom who has stuck with me through thick and thin. All this shit would destroy a mother but she's proud of me, of what I'm doing now and of what I've done in the past. Love you Mom, always remember that.

To everyone at Head-Hunter Books, Martin for his help with the book, John Barnes the computer wizard, Kate on the spell check, Mandy and Kortney answering the phones which are ringing all day long and last but not least, Rory who drives the fork lift at the warehouse. Thanks all of you. A big thank you also to D'Artagnan 56a East St Chichester, West Sussex they supplied my shirt for the front cover of the book, they've a men's clothes shop that sells all the latest gear a shop that every football fan should visit to buy their terrace fashion. Believe me, go there and find out.

CHAPTER ONE

LENNY, LEMMY
WHO GIVES A FUCK?

A story had just been in a local newspaper that a forthcoming television documentary about football hooliganism would feature a well-known football hooligan from the Wolverhampton area and that his name was Lenny. I'd just come back from watching England win 5-1 in a World Cup qualifier out in Germany with a mate of mine whose name is Laney, so I thought it was him. Well, Laney sounds more like Lenny than Gilly, which is how I'm known to everyone that knows me. I was born Gilroy Shaw, but I'm Gilly or Gil to family and friends and to almost everyone else. When I got to the bottom, of the article. In which I so engrossed, there was a photograph of me. Fucking hell. My heart pumped faster and faster and a bead of sweat ran down my forehead. "You're in the brown stuff now my old son" I said to myself. My phone up at my Auntie's house where I was living at the time didn't stop ringing, and in the end, I had to take it off the hook to get some peace and quiet. "Have you seen the papers?" I'd have loved a pound for every time the phone rang and that was the first words out of the callers' mouths. Half the conversation I couldn't recall as I was in another world. My head was spinning and I couldn't think straight. I even thought about fucking off and getting away from it all, maybe grabbing a few of my belongings, slinging them into a holdall, getting some money out of the shoe box under my bed, and fucking off to Spain. Or maybe I should go further afield, maybe Thailand. I could get a job, meet a bird and settle down and maybe get married, but knowing the luck I was having the bird would turn out to be a lady-boy! No fuck it, I know, I'll fuck off and join the French Foreign Legion. I soon got that thought out of my head as I couldn't stand all that regimentation and shouting and screaming and square bashing and taking orders, and I couldn't speak a word of French. No, forget that one. I had to stay and face the music.

The night the programme was due on, I ended up round, Nosher's house. Who's a good mate of mine I must have drove him and his poor wife mad, as I couldn't sit still. I was like a kid on Christmas Eve night I was up and down and made endless visits to the toilet for a piss. I was murder, a fucking nightmare, I was a proper fidget and to tell you the truth I didn't know what to expect and felt a bit of a prick for getting caught out and not knowing it. Still, we sat back on Nosher's settee and the programme got underway. The titles came up with a few lines about how football hooliganism today still plagues football and this they said is the story that football's billion pound industry would rather you did not see. Next up they showed England fans out in Germany for the England game I had been at. "I was out there," I said, pointing to the screen and shouting excitedly Nosher looked at me smiled and nodded his head as if to say alright Gil calm down and the programme then showed English fans standing around peacefully drinking outside bars. Then the programme cuts to show the German police going through their hand-to-hand combat routines in case of any trouble. A British copper at a press conference is shown talking the usual shit about how 537 known troublemakers have been prevented from travelling and how airports and ports were being monitored and were on red alert in an on-going operation. He added in reassuring tones that he very much doubted that large numbers of known troublemakers would be travelling to the game. Someone wasn't telling the truth, has the programme then showed street clashes between rival German and English fans. Bottles and glasses were flying through the air as the German Old Bill desperately tried to restore order and in amongst it appeared a familiar figure. I can't say a familiar face because they had my boat race fazed over but I recognised my body, voice and clothes and they were calling me "Lenny, and said that I was a well-known Wolverhampton Wanderers hooligan". Lenny? Where did they get that name from, fucking Lenny? I was shown wearing a rather fetching pair of shorts and a light blue Stone Island top, and I could be seen waving my arm in the air and shouting "they've only got this, let's fucking do them". I look across at Nosher and his wife and I cringe. They look back, smile, but don't say a word. The programme then describes me as "another veteran of Euro 2000". I can then be heard, shouting at the England fans around me, to "Get out the pub and fucking do 'em" I'm then described as a Top Boy, a category C hooligan, and that I'm one of the leading figures in Wolves Subway Army. I look across at Nosher. "Subway Army", I say, "they were about twenty years before my time". He laughs, "don't worry Gil it's only telly Gill, it's not true" and we both laugh. The programme goes on to say that they can't show my face in full for legal reasons but they continue to film me with their hidden camera. They show me talking about the row with the Germans. "Will there be any more trouble?" asks the prick with the hidden camera. Like a cunt I reply "yea, all day". The voice on the programme then says, "Lenny's prediction seems to be accurate" as it then shows more trouble between rival fans. "Fuck me" I say to Nosher, "they've got it in for me". "I thought that copper just said that all the troublemakers had been banned from travelling," Nosher's wife said scratching her head, a bit bemused by it all.

The programme then moved away from the events in Germany and on to the domestic scene and showed a Nottingham Forest mob in a south London pub as they plan their travels to the New Den. They speak to a few ex hooligans on why trouble still goes on and show Millwall fans having it and fighting with the Old Bill. Names of various clubs flash up across the screen as the violence between certain teams is described. Next up is the Walsall V Wolves fixture and the geezer with the hidden camera is shown being stopped and searched by the Old Bill. He embarrassingly 'as to own up to having a hidden camera about his person and he then tells the coppers what he's up to, he's allowed on his way and, surprise surprise, next up on the screen again is good old me. A few of the Wolves boys have stumbled across Mr. Spielberg with his hidden camera still rolling, and he shits himself as we give him a squeeze. I ask him a few questions and he mumbles and stutters about how he'd met me in Germany, he's shitting himself big time and we know he's up to something but didn't quite know what. If we'd had given him a slap we would have been classed as bullies, this geezer was a fucking divvey little weed he was trembling and shaking so I bid him a good night and there was no violence as he went on his way unharmed the police are in close attendance as they watch from across the street. The programme then talks about hooligans not wearing shirts or colours but wearing designer gear. Fuck me, that quote must have come from a professor at some two bob university who aint got an ounce of common sense and who knows fuck all about football or football fans, trouble is this sort of quote then gets filtered down to some police spokesman who then uses it. It's just a vicious circle, not the fans but the bollocks spoken about us. West Brom away at the Hawthorns is where I'm shown next. What happens, which isn't shown on the film, is that about sixty of us have come out from the back of the ground and go out onto Halfords Lane where we are hanging around for the rest of our lot, to come out onto the street. Prick Brains with the hidden camera 'as somehow managed to follow me, and a few of the other lads as we are fed up waiting and head off up the road. The Old Bill behind us are holding the Albion fans back but as more and more of them come pouring out of the stadium they start having trouble holding them back. People are getting impatient as they want to beat the crowds back to the local train stations and tram stops, women and children at the front are getting crushed and suddenly the human dam bursts and bodies are in amongst us. On the film, which misses the mad rush for the station, you hear a voice telling the viewers that "Lenny is amongst this mob" but it's nighttime and the pictures are very dark and shadowy and at this point, it's hard to make out whose who. The man with the hidden video camera is unbeknown to me following in my footsteps the microphone and the camera pick up a man walking beside me then you hear a voice say. "You Baggies? " You can't hear my reply but the word "yes" comes up in subtitles shown on the screen, in fact I replied, "whatever". The film not very clearly, then shows a man falling down and someone in the crowd shouting "they're behind us". The police rush in, and the hidden camera and the man holding it are pushed up against the wall. The programme then goes on to say that I'd punched a person to the floor. You couldn't tell who was who it was that dark. I look at Nosher and he shakes his head. I'm lost for words, embarrassed by it all and they then cut from the West Brom game and show me sitting with a coach load of Wolves' fans pulling up outside the New Den at Millwall. Again there's no fighting, just a bit of verbals, and a few wankers signs, which is something that every visiting away fan has been through while watching their team away from home, again my face is blanked out. The programme carries on a bit more and when it ends, Nosher's wife gets up to put the kettle on. There is complete silence and I think we're all in shock. I get up and bid Nosher and his missus goodnight but they don't say a word. A hundred and one things go through my mind has I make my way back up to my Auntie's house. I put the key in the door and let myself in I close the door behind me and she's already standing in the hallway waiting for me. "You should be ashamed of yourself," she says staring angrily at me before I could answer her she turns her back on me and walks away. What could I say? I went straight to my room and laid on the bed. I just couldn't sleep and I just knew it was only a matter of time before the Old Bill came around and paid me a visit. The phone never stopped ringing for days has I stayed hidden from the world cocooned in my bedroom all I could hear was Auntie's voice telling whoever it was calling that I wasn't in. Good old Auntie. In her own way I suppose she was still being protective even though she was angry. She was probably worried about what the neighbours might think or might be saying about us.

After a few days I was up and out and about and ready to face the world and the shit it would throw at me I just felt people looking at me and some even blatantly pointed at me from across the street. I had complete strangers shouting "Lenny" at me or the classic line "we know it's you". It was has if these people knew me it was as if these people owned part of my life, or even shared my life with me. It was madness. I'd been stitched up on T.V. and had been portrayed as some kind of monster, it was Reality, Stitch Up T.V. at it's worst or for some sad cunts at it's best and it seemed the public now wanted their pound of flesh. I'd come into their front rooms through the television screens and I had to answer to them. One bloke even shouted out "alright Lemmy?" I shook my head, "fucking Lemmy". I thought, the only Lemmy I'd ever heard of was the lead singer and bass guitarist from the heavy rock band Motorhead. He once sang and played on "Silver Machine" a hit for cosmic rock band Hawkwind, but he looked nothing like me and he was a good twenty years older, and had long, greasy, lank, dark hair, a big bushy moustache, and side burns and had quite a few large warts, pimples, and boils on his face. "Alright Lemmy?" What fucking programme had this cunt been watching? I'd been on a programme about football hooligans, not the fucking "Old Grey Whistle Test," or "Top of the Pops." Days and then weeks passed by, and I still hadn't had the dreaded tap on the shoulder or the front door coming in at half five in the morning so I decided to go to the next home game at the Molineux. I knew I'd get a lot of stick off the boys, I half expected that and all the piss taking. What I didn't expect though was a couple of our Old Bill being sarcastic and in truth being threatening. "Alright big man, how ya doing?" "Do you want to fight me, do you want to try and hit me from behind?" I had these and a few other snide comments thrown at me but I just ignored them. I knew if I dared to have taken answered them back and to have taken the bait then it would have been arms up the back, handcuffs on and thrown into the back of a police wagon. They would have loved to have nicked me just smiling at them gave them the hump even more.

The days and weeks went by and our local paper still carried on running stories about the Subway Army and me. They couldn't even get that right. The Subway Army had disbanded over twenty years ago. Still, you know what newspapers are like when it comes to reporting on football fans. They love to come up with a name, a tag. They love to sensationalise a story. You can't have the truth getting in the way of a good story can you? They can't just write about fans from Chelsea or West Ham or Millwall or Man. United. These fans according to the media have to be members of the Headhunters or the Inter City firm or the Bushwhackers or the Treatment or the Red Army and as for being members of a football gang. How do you become a member? How do you join? Do you have to pay a fee and if so, is it weekly or monthly subs? Is there a secretary? A meeting hall? How do you get into these all-exclusive member-only football gangs?" and they all seem to have more secrets than the Masons, you know, funny handshakes and one leg of your trousers rolled up at strange private initiation ceremonies Aint that the sort of organisation you'd get a police officer or a newspaper editor joining? Anyway, back to me. Sky News got in touch and wanted to do an interview, you know, like me give my side of events. They wanted my account of what went on but I decided to give that a miss.

   After a month or so I decided to book a holiday out in Crete. I'd received a letter from Bob Morrissey, the head of security at Wolves, telling me that in the light of recent events it was best for all parties concerned that until future notice I was to stay away from Molineux. Well, with words to that effect anyway. I'd never met the bloke in my life but with due effect I was banned so I needed a holiday. A mate of mine that worked at Birmingham airport gave me a tip off that if I tried to leave the country then I would be arrested, under a new government legislation aimed at stamping out football violence, the police had the power to stop me from travelling abroad. Well, they had to catch me first before they could stop me and after all, I was only going on holiday to lay in the sun, not to organise a punch up between, Crete Rovers and Corfu Town Albion. The problem was the World Cup Finals were just about to start out in Japan and the Daily Mirror newspaper didn't help when they ran a story about how I claimed to be "The Baddest Hooligan in Britain". They went on to write how the world's former number one player, Diego Maradona, had been banned from Japan because of his conviction for cocaine abuse yet "gang leader Shaw who has been banned from football matches for 11 of the last 14 years and whose most recent exclusion order expires just in time for the World Cup, has been planning his trip to the finals in Japan and Korea for months". Like fuck I had, I had no intention of going to the World Cup and I'd not even spoken to any newspaper, let alone anyone from The Daily Mirror. They also claimed that I'd bragged to them how I'd travelled to England International games abroad by flying from Scottish airports and that I'd also boasted that I'd been done for hooliganism more times than anyone else in Britain. They went on to say that "the father of three had been a hooligan for more than 20 years". It was all bollocks. I was going on holiday with my mate Danny Slater, to Crete, which even by my geography was nowhere near Japan or Korea. I was off for two weeks in the sun, not a month to the Land of the Rising Sun. I soon found out it was me mate Abbo who'd given the interview to The Mirror. Not me, I'd not spoken two words to them. Still, I didn't hold it against Abbo and he's still a good pal of mine to this day. Me and Danny didn't want our holiday fucked up by getting our collars felt at Birmingham Airport so we got me mum to drive us up to Glasgow where we'd bought single flight tickets out to Crete. It went as sweet as a nut and we had two lovely weeks in the sun and on arrival back at Birmingham on our original air tickets we gave a little wave and a smile to the Old Bill that were still waiting for us to travel out, as we were arriving back. You should have seen the looks on their faces! It said it all. The word "bastards" was etched on their boat races. We'd fucked them good and proper; we'd enjoyed our two weeks in Malia. A couple of times I was recognised as "that geezer off the telly" but all in all it was a nice break. The World Cup tournament was still going on when my son Adam moved in with me into our new house in Bilston. I redecorated it from top to bottom and I was just putting the finishing touches to the front room skirting boards when I saw a police van pull up outside. I could see they're from the O.S.U. (the Operations Support Unit). I put down the paintbrush I was using and went to the front door, which was already half open, without knocking, two policemen walk straight into the hallway. Immediately Starsky and Hutch set about playing good cop – bad cop. "Sign this," says the stroppy one thrusting a piece of paper into my hand. "I see you're busy decorating," says Mr. Nice Guy. I nod my head as I read the document I've been handed. "Had a lot to do?" asks Good Cop looking up the stairs and rubbing his hand along the top of the smooth gleaming freshly glossed banister rail. I bet he watches "Changing Rooms" I'm thinking to myself. Mr. Stroppy butts in. "Read it and sign it". He says handing me a pen "Hang on, hang on, let's read it first" I say reading through it slowly and trying to work out and trying to understand what's written on the paper, and from what I can gather, and reading through it quite quickly, it's some sort of summons to go to Court to receive a Banning Order. It's been around three months since the programme on T.V. and to be honest I'd expected the Old Bill around sooner than now. Mr good copper bids me farewell like he is a close mate of mine that has just popped by to say hello. Mr Grumpy just grunts as he looks at my signature and places the paperwork in his jacket pocket. He looks as pleased as punch in his own unhappy way. I closed the front door and watch from the front room window as the van slowly drives away and up the road, and out of sight. I let out a deep breath of air and collapsed backwards onto the plastic dustsheet that's covering the settee. It seems like a ton weight has just been lifted off of my shoulders. A sort of relief washes over me now maybe I can get on with my life but football has always been in my blood. I'd been watching the Wolves for over 20 years so would it be that easy to stop going? I closed my eyes and let my head hit the back of the settee. Soon thoughts and memories of my early years came flooding back, but how did it all end up like this?

CHAPTER TWO

GYPSY KID

I was born on the 25th January 1968 in Wednesbury, which is a suburb of West Bromwich, in Portland House, a private nursing home. My Mum and Dad were living in Wolverhampton Street, Darlaston at that time. Later on, I was joined by my sister Annette who is a couple of years younger than I am. Dad was an engineer in a local factory and Mum was from a large Gypsy travelling family, who were a combination of the Boswells and the Smiths, who were well known in the area. We lived with my Nan and my mum's sisters in a big house. I had a very happy childhood and everyone got along fine but when I was about five, I remember my Dad having a bad accident at work, which resulted in him losing his foot. From what I can remember, I think it was crushed in a machine. He later had an artificial foot fitted and it wasn't long after that that Mum and him split up and finally got divorced. They used to have some right rows and fights. I remember he turned up at me Nan's house one night steaming drunk and obviously looking for a fight. My Nan, my Mum and her sisters went out and give it to him big time and after he'd copped a few right handers and kicks up the arse they chased him up the road. He couldn't run that fast so he took a good few whacks around the head. They came back to the house laughing as he hobbled off into the night. "That'll teach him," said Nan, "he won't be back". And he never did. I don't think I ever saw him after that little incident, he would have learnt not to fuck about with Gypsy women that's for sure.

While Mum went out to work me and me sister were brought up by

Nan who was a real old fashioned lady who didn't stand for any nonsense. She was strong and protective and always called me "my lad" and I loved her to bits. I knew I was in trouble though when she looked at me, waved her finger at me, and beckoned me with a "get here mother's cunt". I knew then I was in big trouble. She kept herself and the house spotless. She wasn't one for giving you loads of hugs and kisses as showing you affection wasn't her way, but you still knew that you were loved and wanted. She was a big, strong, gypsy woman and was the biggest crook God ever put on this earth. She pulled so many strokes and if anyone knocked on the door selling a bit of hooky gear, she'd buy it off them. The entire local thieves vagabonds and Herbert's treated her with the utmost respect. They never called her by her first name, which was Dinah, they always called her Mrs. Smith as she was so well respected. At that time me Mum was working in one of the local factories and me Nan and mum's sister, me Auntie Kath, looked after me and me sister and we were spoilt rotten. Me Auntie Kath was the one who showered us with affection. She would sling her arms around us and crush us and smother us with cuddles and kisses. She was so much like me mum and they both showed us so much love.

Soon it was time for me to start school, no more playing out in the street, it was time to go off and learn how to read and write. My first school was Greenacres Nursery and the first day I was taken by a neighbour, Iris, with her two sons, Michael and Kevin. They were a bit older than me and were in the infants' school, already. The first day there I was as sick as a dog and the school had to get in touch with me Nan to come and get me. She was at home looking after me sister because mum was out at work. I'd eaten a load of chocolate marshmallows during the break and I honked me guts up. I never told anyone what made me sick but I was kept off school for a few months after that, everyone thought I had some mystery virus or something. I was well pleased to be back home with Nan and me sister. I didn't care if I never went back to school again, fuck learning to read and write and learning to count and times tables and all that shit I loved the home life. In the end the school sent someone round to say that I had to be back at school as I was having valuable time off. I reluctantly went back and made loads of friends but it was in and around the house that I was happiest. My uncles and aunties were always popping in and out and I loved nothing more than sitting around the burning fire in the front room listening to their tales and stories. Gypsy folk can tell a good tale. Herbert, mum's brother, had died when I was about three and I just about remember him but there was also uncle Roy and uncle Arthur who was known to everyone for some reason as Archie and I had an uncle Gilly, who I was named after. My Granddad and great Granddad were also named Gilroy or Gilly for short. It's a good old Gypsy name. I also had Mums sisters Aunties Kathy, Mary and Rhoda. Every day the men would go out calling or "totting" as they were rag-and-bone men. They didn't go out on a horse and cart in the old traditional way, but in an old Transit van. They'd go door-to-door knocking and give a gift of a cheap toy in a bag for any wares given to them by the house owner. Me uncles always looked after me and were very kind but between themselves they would often bicker and argue and one might not talk to the other for weeks, or even months, over something trivial. It was always the smallest of things that would spark a row off, but then that's travellers for ya. They're not happy unless they're arguing or fighting with someone, or amongst themselves, I'd sometimes go out with me uncles and clear factories of all the scrap metal. My job was to bag it up in separate bags, like copper in one bag, lead in another, brass in another, then they'd take it in, get it weighed up at the scrap man's and bung me a couple of bob. They educated me how to duck and dive and on how to earn a living. Besides bunging me a few quid they also had to sort Nan out her share.

As a kid aged about six or seven I remember me Uncle Gilly taking me out into the country out near Cannock and showing me a field and in it were about fifty horses. "There ya go Gilly my boy" he said, patting me on the head, as I lent over the barbed wire fence "twenty four of them horses are yours". Fucking hell I was over the moon I must have been the richest six year old traveller kid in the Midlands. Every chance I had I'd pester me uncles to take me back up there and I'd ride the horses bare backed. I done things Gorger kids (none Gypsy folk) could only dream of and even at that young age I loved life. We had our own language, (Romany) which only we and other travellers could understand, and I felt I was wiser, and more streetwise than other kids were my age. I remember going into cafes with my uncles and tucking into piles of grub. We had money, horses, trucks and vans. I even had a couple of big Alsatian dogs which were kept in the back yard with me uncles' couple of Jack Russells and greyhounds. The dogs or Juks as we call them are never allowed indoors. Keeping dogs and cats indoors is what Gorger folk do travellers don't have any animals inside their homes and Gorgers have the neck to call us dirty bastards and one thing you wont see is us kissing a dog or cat. All the dogs had the same name, "Mush". When you called them it was "come here Mush" and "fetch Mush, "fuck off Mush". How they never got confused I'll never know. However, they were treated well and were always fed, watered and exercised.

The years had gone by now and my dad was well and truly out of our lives. I'd grown to hate him, not because he wasn't around but just from the stories mum had told me about how he'd knocked her about and how he'd spend all the housekeeping and his wages on other birds and boozing in the pub.

I was about eight when I first got interested in football. I played with other kids out in the street. We'd have about twenty aside and use jumpers or coats as goalposts. I remember one of the Asian kids that lived up the road getting the ball passed to him and him doing a running commentary out loud which went something like this, "Jeff Astle gets the ball, he beats one, then two, he rounds the keeper and the ball hits the back of the net"! "Jeff Astle" I'm thinking, " he's the big bloke that plays centre-forward for the Baggies and England". Abdul don't look nothing like him, but that was it, I soon realised that with football you could dream, you could be anyone you wanted and that was the beauty of the game. Those street games were crazy and would go on for hours with no one it seemed keeping or even bothered what the score was.

I suppose the first team that I ever supported or look out for, was "The Villa". I'd broken into the school football team and kids were wearing the scarves and woollen hats in the colours of their favourite teams, the popular ones being West Brom, Wolves, Aston Villa, Man. Utd. A lot of the kids seemed to support Villa and me Auntie Kath bless her sent me a birthday card with Andy Gray, Dennis Mortimer and a few of the Aston Villa players pictured on it. I wasn't allowed to watch "Match of the Day" on BBC 1 on a Saturday night or "The Big Match" on a Sunday afternoon. "What do ya want to watch that shit for?" was what I'd get if I asked to watch football on T.V., but that all changed when I got a black and white portable in me bedroom. Wednesday night was Sportsnight on the T. V. and I could watch the highlights from that evening's games. I suppose I was glory hunting a bit at the time as Villa had quite a successful team then and always seemed to be on the telly. I'd see kids at school with claret and blue Villa scarves on and I'd been given a little, metal, Villa badge, which I wore with pride on my school jacket. Even at my tender age me and me sister were taught by Nan to keep ourselves and our rooms spotlessly clean. All the family had been through it and if me uncles didn't keep the yard clean she used to crack 'em one.

When I was about ten me mum's friend or work mate, Gary, who she worked with at the factory, took me to see Wolves play Liverpool at the Molineux. I was sworn to secrecy by me Mum that I was going to a match with Gary because me Nan if she found out wouldn't have approved of her having a boyfriend, even at my Mum's age and even though she had two children, she was frightened of Nan. Therefore, mum had to play it down by telling me and Nan that her and Gary were just friends. Anyway, I met them both after work and Gary took me off on the number 79 bus to the Molineux which is the home of the world famous Wolverhampton Wanderers. The nearer we got to the ground the slower the bus went due to the heavy traffic and all the people walking in its path. A couple of stops before the ground we jumped off and walked, as there was thousands of people milling around and traffic was at a virtual standstill. We got to the turnstiles, Gary handed the man working them a pound, and we both squeeze through on the same click. Nan would be proud of him and me I'm thinking. Inside the noise hit me. We're playing Liverpool who is a massive side that's won nearly every trophy there is to win and have some top stars in their side many I've seen on telly and in the pages of the football mags me mates bring into school both sets of fans are trying to out-sing one another. I've heard quite a few the songs being sung before but the fans have changed the words. Old and the latest pop songs are now football songs as they echo around the ground. I look around as the swaying crowds push me backwards and forwards. But Gary keeps a close eye on me and I know he wont let me get crushed It's dark and the floodlights are on and a misty steam seems to be slowly moving across the green pitch. I'm so excited. Gary tells me we're standing on the North Bank, which is the family section. I feel comfortable with him, not shy at all and he seems to be a decent bloke. Liverpool win 1-0 with an Alan Hansen goal and from then on I was hooked even though Wolves lost I made my mind up there and then that from that day I was going to be a Wolves fan, fuck the Villa, this is the team for me.

Next day at school the rest of the kids gathered around me as I told them I'd been to see the Wolves play and they were now my team. I got home from school and slung me Villa gear, including the hat and scarf that Auntie Kath had knitted me, into the back of the wardrobe. I soon became John Richards, the legendary Wolves centre forward, in our street kick-about's.It wasn't until I was about fourteen and at Mosley Park Secondary School that I went to a game again. A lad called Ken Till, who was three years older than me and worked as a milkman, used to talk to me about football and Wolves. I was friendly with his younger brother and his Mum and my Nan were real good friends. I was now at that age that I was just discovering fashion so out went the brogue Dealer boots and the braces, and in came the Pringle and Lyle and Scot jumpers, Pierre Sangan and Puma and Addidas trainers which were all in and were all worn by me. I had also changed my taste in music. I'd been brought up on a diet of rock and roll and Elvis and the family thought I was half divvy when I started listening to new bands like Spandau Ballet, Depeche Mode and The Human League, and watching all the latest bands and groups on Top of the Pops. "You can't tell whose a man and whose a woman these days, they're all fucking shit" Nan would say as she popped her head around my bedroom door and caught me singing and dancing along to the groups on telly. I daren't answer her back, as I would gingerly put the airbrush down that I'd been using as a microphone.

Me uncle Gilly was a keen footballer who'd played for local side Bilston and he had once had trials at Wolves. He used to tell me he wasn't really bothered about making it as a pro because there was more money in scrap metal than being a footballer. I started going to a few games with Ken but all he liked doing was clapping and singing and waving the silk Wolves scarf he had tied around his wrist above his head, whereas me, I was a cheeky fucker that liked standing next to the away fans and giving them the two fingered salute and the wankers sign. Ken even dressed like a boring cunt. He'd wear big, heavy, purple Pod shoes, the ones with the animal tracks on the sole and the compass in the heel. He was a nice lad who wouldn't hurt a fly but he wasn't really my cup of tea and after a few seasons of going with him it was time to move on and find some new mates. The team was doing shit on the pitch and we'd gone from the First Division right through to almost being relegated to Division 4. We were awful, absolute shit.

I left school at 16 and went to work on a Y.T.S. scheme in a D.I.Y. hardware shop in Dudley. I was on £25 a week selling tins of paint and nails and screws. I was the general dogsbody who had to stack the shelves make the tea go and get the sandwiches and sweep up. The shop was right near Dudley Zoo and the jobs I was given could have been done by the chimpanzees out of the nearby monkey house. What's the old saying? "You pay peanuts and you get monkeys". They could have saved the government £25 a week; fucking hell it was a boring job. I rolled up 40 minutes late the first morning because I didn't know the times of the two buses I needed to catch to get there. I hated it and only lasted two months, as I wasn't used to taking senseless orders. I'd sit on the bus on the way to work thinking there had to be an easier way of life and that the people there were just morbid dickheads. Nan was chuffed to bits when I went home with my first week's pay and showed her the little brown envelope containing my hard earned cash and the good thing was I got to keep it all to myself. Mum and Nan never asked for a penny for housekeeping. I was a good saver so I used to poke a few quid away each week, which meant I could now buy all the latest fashions. I was into Patrick clothes and Kickers shoes and even bought myself a pink pair. I started going to a local youth club and it was around this time that I seemed to be moving away from the travellers' life style in which I'd been cocooned all my life I had to get out and broaden my horizons, stretch my wings, go on foreign holidays, see different places, meet different types of people. It was time for me to move on, it didn't take long, after just a couple of visits to the club, I met Tracey Shinton through my mate Dave Walters, who we all knew as Dava. He was a good-looking lad and was a right ladies' man. The girls loved him he wore all the latest gear and the pair of us had a lot in common. Like me, his dad had fucked off when he was young. The beautiful Tracey was sixteen, lived local and was a normal, looking girl. I was still a virgin and had only met girls like Tracey when I was having a wank, one night to my surprise she invited me, Dava, Pete Matthews and a few other lads back to her house which was empty as her mum and dad ran a pub and were hardly ever at home. "Go on" said Dava, "get in there". "Why don't you?" I asked has Tracey sorted out some records to put on. "I've been there before," said Dava, "you have a go" he smiled. "Why don't you?" I asked again. "Because Gil, her fanny stinks" he said, and we all fell about laughing. I made some excuse about wanting to ask Tracey something in private and we went upstairs to her bedroom. Before I could shut the door behind me she had pulled the bedroom curtains and was stripped down to her bra and knickers. I pulled my pants down and fumbled in my pocket for a Johnnie bag, which I slipped onto my 14 inches of throbbing gristle, well 12 inches anyway, o.k. I'm lying, six! She slipped her knickers and bra off and threw them onto the floor and I pulled my shirt off, kicked my socks off, and climbed on top of her. She pulled the blanket over both of us as I tried to get me Cory up her, no kissing, no foreplay; I was straight in there. She moaned and let out a deep breath as I entered her. I was half expecting and waiting for the stench to rise up but had to quickly forget about that and hold on for dear life as she pumped up and down on me dick it was like being in a wild west rodeo show. I was getting into it now and was feeling well pleased with myself as I banged away when suddenly the door burst open and the boys came rushing in laughing their heads off. They began slapping my bare arse and saying "go on boy". I could have died, I was so embarrassed. I hadn't even come my lot. I was up got dressed and we all left, leaving the poor girl all alone in a state of undress. We laughed as we walked off home and I thought to myself, "I've done it, I've lost my virginity". I was a man now, a proper, fully-fledged man. I felt great. No more wanking alone for me from now on. The one thing that did worry me though was if me Mum found out. You see Tracey worked with Mum and I didn't know how Mum would react if she found out that her little soldier had been shagging one of her work colleagues. Mum has a good sense of humour but I would have got some untold stick.

After my John-and-Yoko-style, love-in with Tracey my outlook on life seemed to change. I was at a Wolves game and I saw a group of Cockney lads in clothes I'd never seen before. They had on Lacoste, Robe de Kappa, and Ellesse designer labels which none of our lot were wearing around this time. I started knocking around with Darren Butler and another fella called Gutcher. They were from around Bilston and the three of us used to watch the Wolves mob, the Subway Army, in action in and around the ground. They were a legendary mob that got their name from ambushing rival fans in the subway near to the ground. One of the helpers at the youth club was a known face with them and he would tell us bits and pieces about what the boys had been up to and how when we'd played Liverpool they'd smashed the scousers all over the station forecourt. He also told us about the time they'd gone into Leeds' main boozer, The "Peacock", and had it with Leeds and smashed them to pieces something not many teams around that time done. We'd hang on his every word and he was someone that had our total respect. Over the weeks the people we nodded to on the South Bank would come over and have a chat and our circle began to expand. We even went to a few away games, all funded by my ducking and diving and ability to earn a few quid. At this time, the ground was being re-developed, the John Ireland stand later became the Steve Bull stand, all the lads then moved to the old enclosure and I remember the Chelsea firm going in the seats opposite us, and they looked impressive. They were their lads and most of them were grown men, and they stood up and sang "One Man Went to Mow". They did look the part and outside we soon found out, as it went off everywhere with them, they were as game as fuck, Arsenal once done the same thing but not on the scale of Chelsea. Then I met a man who, I suppose, helped shape my football going days.

CHAPTER THREE

MEETING FINGLES

Dave Powers was known to everyone at "The Wolves" as Fingles. He was about twenty-five stone with slightly greasy, curly hair and was a good fifteen years older than me. He was a main face in the firm who ran coaches to away games and you'd always find him wearing a white Benetton top with a blue stripe through the middle. After the Subway Army ended, Fingles and his boys from Darlaston came to the forefront. I got chatting to him once at a home game and he asked me and a couple of my mates if we fancied going on his coach to the next away game. "Come with us kid," he said, and me and me mates couldn't believe it. The great man had actually spoke to us, it was like David Bowie asking you to do a duet with him on his new album or Elvis's manager phoning you up and asking you to stand in for "The King" at one of his Las Vegas gigs. We were made up.

Fingles ran a coach, which would do multi pickups from Tipton and stop at various pubs picking up people along the way. The coach was an old banger and Cranktock Coaches was the name of them. Fingles would charge between £4 and £6 depending on where we were travelling to for the game. They were great fun and we used to have a right laugh. Fingles would sit at the front, just behind the driver. He was like a strict teacher and we were like naughty school children sitting behind him and pulling faces. We would have all sorts on the coach, beer monsters, hooligan wannabies, and out and out head cases. The beer monsters would carry on cases and cases of beer and bottles of wine and spirits. We went everywhere on that clapped out coach, London,

Brighton, Portsmouth and he didn't give a fuck who came as long as they paid. Me, Bowie, (not David) Little Ray, Hilda, we were all the same age and we loved it. We went to Blackburn Rovers on the coach once and pulled up outside a back-street pub and all piled off, inside it was decked out in Blackburn's colours, with Shirts and scarves and rosettes and team photos all pinned up on the wall it was a proper football pub. The guv'nor started to serve the first few off the coach with pints of beer, no problem. A few Blackburn lads in the back of the bar had seen us come in and one dickhead amongst them chucks a glass in our direction. That was it, it goes off mental. The place was trashed, windows were put in, with broken glass, everywhere furniture was smashed into firewood, and the place was a complete wreck. We all managed to get out and get away before the Old Bill turned up but down at the ground there was more trouble, not with Blackburn's mob or with the Old Bill, but with Fingles who was so fat he couldn't fit through the turnstiles and they had to let him in through the main gate. We were in hysterics as his baggy El cheapo jeans had slipped down at the back as he waddled in and he was showing an ample cleavage of bum cheeks. He was no sooner in than he was straight up to the food counter for a hot steak and kidney pie. He loved his grub did Fingles. It seemed he always had some sort of pie or pasty squashed into his rather large, porky, sausage-like fingers. His chops would be constantly on the move, either slurping from a can of beer or digesting a spot of greasy grub. He was the real life Desperate Dan, a real salad dodger but he was loved by all, a real character. One thing, if it went off he'd never let you down. He'd stand and fight but to be honest he didn't have a lot of choice, as he was too fat to move. On the way back from games we would pull into the motorway services and the coach would empty as we went off for a piss stop or a spot of shopping. We'd rob the shop of sweets; crisps, sandwiches and drinks, and the more romantic ones amongst us would grab a stuffed teddy bear or some soft toy for their girlfriends or wives back home.

If we went to a midland derby us, young lot would go by train and meet up with Fingles and his beer monsters in a pub in the city centre. One particular game at Coventry we met up with them and after a while, the young lot were bored so we went looking for some action. There was about twenty of us and after looting the fruit and fag machines in a few different pubs we were walking up the road counting our haul when we stumbled across a mob of about seventy Coventry. They ran at us and we went in every direction. We were only young kids and this Coventry mob were grown men. I split from the others and ran down a side road but I could hear them behind me getting closer and closer. I daren't look behind my heart was beating nine to the dozen. My chest was ready to explode as I try to gulp down the air needed to keep me going. I kept looking straight ahead and it's now every boy for himself. I can hear them right behind me I can now feel their breath on the back of my neck I feel like a Gazelle being chased by a angry and hungry lion the next thing I know I'm sprawled out on the floor and the bastards are all over me punching and kicking me, self survival kicks in and I curl up in a ball but has I look down I can see my Farrah trousers have been ripped on both knees, I'm gutted they've my favourite pair of trousers. After a while, the kicks and punches stop and I look through my bruised and swollen fingers, which have been protecting my head, and I can see my attackers have fucked off and I'm all-alone. I stand up shakily look down at myself, and half smile. At least I'm in one piece but my head is fucking sore and thumping like mad where I've been whacked so many times but there's no blood. I tuck my shirt back into my ripped trousers and set off to find Fingles and the older lads we'd left behind in the pub at the top of the road. There's three or four of our lads who were chased with me just picking themselves up off the floor and a couple look half concussed as we stagger back up towards the pub, we tell the older lads inside what's gone on and they quickly drink up as we leave as one mob and go looking for revenge. However, we don't see a mob of Coventry for the rest of the day. Back home word soon spread that I'd had the shit kicked out of me at Coventry but by the time I'd embellished the story a little and bent the truth a bit it sounded like I'd taken on the whole of Coventry's mob on my own and come out of it quite lightly. I'd propelled myself right up there as one of the chaps Come the next week I'd forgotten about my beating and was still up for going to football the incident at Coventry didn't put me off of going one bit.

Around this time Fingles's coach firm and us young lot sort of went our separate ways and parted company. Our lot from Bilston sort of mobbed up with the Wednesfield lot as our numbers just grew, as different young up and coming faces from the surrounding Wolverhampton areas seemed to come together. We all started to trust one another, over the course of time, we just gelled and bonded together, and it was strange how it all came about. For a few weeks or months we'd just nodded at one another, then it was a smile, and then eventually a "hello mate" and then you'd see the same faces at away games and a friendship would be forged. It's funny how these things come about.

Around this time I'd had my hair dyed blonde and cut into a wedge. I was a sort of New Romantic and was listening to Duran Duran and Spandau Ballet. Their videos influenced my hairdo and dress sense but looking back now I cringe at the thought of what I must have looked like, but then again I wasn't alone. There were thousands of people influenced into dressing like, total pricks. Anyway dressed exactly like Simon Le Bon in the "Rio " or "Girls on film " video I went over to watch Walsall play Liverpool in a Cup game. Inside the ground, a wall collapsed as thousands of Liverpool fans pushed forward and spilled onto the pitch. Outside afterwards it was going off and the Old Bill grabbed me, nicked me, and charged me with a section five, which is using threatening words and behaviour. I went to Walsall Magistrates Court a few weeks later and I received a conditional discharge. The copper who arrested me had then stood up in court and come up with the most amazing story I'd ever heard it was total bollocks pure shit and I couldn't believe he was talking about me. I just sat there shaking my head in disbelief, as it was all crap. I just happened to be in the wrong place at the wrong time and he had just grabbed the nearest person to him, which unfortunately just happened to be me. As a travelling boy I'd always been told just what lying cunts the gavvers were "never trust them" me Nan used to say and all me uncles and aunties would all agree and it seemed they were right. There were three other Wolves fans in the dock that day who were all bound over to keep the peace. I went home and me Uncle Gilly said he was ashamed of me but when I told him what had gone on I think he changed his mind.

Around this time I'd also become a bit of a stud. I don't know if it was me blonde hair but I became fanny mad and I was doing very well with the minge and I was chasing birds all over the place. I'd lost a bit of weight and I was feeling good and confident. When I reached, eighteen I had my first real, serious relationship with a girl. I went to school with her and she was a year younger than I was. Her name was Mandy Chapman and she came from Portobella, which was just up the road from Bilston. I hadn't seen her for years and one night I bumped into her in the Cleveland Arms where I used to drink with a few of the lads from football. She was a pretty little thing and was working as a hairdresser. My wedge haircut had now grown long at the back and I had a bit of a mullet, a sort of Chris Waddle hairdo. I remember seeing him and Tottenham's Glen Hoddle singing their poxy song "Diamond Lights" on "Top of the Pops" with their sleeves on their cotton jackets pulled up to the elbows in a sort of "Miami Vice" T.V. cop look along with their mullet hairstyles which at the time seemed to be the footballers' coiffured look. Mandy and I got chatting and we arranged to meet. I knew she fancied me by the way she was acting and talking and I could just tell by her body language that I was well in. The group of lads I was knocking about with were getting a bit of a reputation and a bit of a name for themselves and maybe that's what attracted her to me. The night I was meant to meet her I was in two minds whether to turn up or not or go out in my Opel Manta for a spin around the streets and show off. That car was my pride and joy even though I'd been driving out on the roads since I was about fourteen, like a lot of Gypsy kids I was shown how to drive at a very young age. I must have been taught the right way because when I was old enough I passed my driving test at the first attempt. Anyway, I changed my mind at the last minute and set off to meet her and I was late picking her up from her house. Her mum told me she'd gone off to the Royal Oak pub so I drove over there and walked in she saw and jumped up from her chair "Did you forget me?" she said. Wrapping her arms around my neck.

"No, I've come for ya" I replied and from then on we were a couple. She was from a very respectable family and I loved her so much. I even moved in with her after a few months and we lived happily at her parents' house. Her Mum and Dad had recently split up, I was made to feel more than welcome, and they never once asked me for a penny towards the housekeeping or to pay towards any bills. I wasn't in any steady employment and all the money I made from ducking and diving was me own money but nearly every other weekend me and her would go off up to Blackpool for a dirty weekend but that was mostly in the summer when the football season had finished. After about eighteen months we rented a flat together and for the first time in my life I had to break with tradition and help with paying bills, rent and food. I'd lived at me Mums and Nan's for years without parting with a penny and now I was being told I had to help- out financially, anyway I soon got used to it, although initially it hurt.

One morning at six o'clock the front door came crashing in and the Old Bill came steaming up the stairs, they drag us out of bed and turned the place upside down and anything with Wolverhampton Wanderers on it was bagged up and taken away. I was arrested in what was part of what the police code-named "Operation Growth". The growth stood for "Get rid of Wolves Troublesome Hooligans". I was taken to a police station and charged, overall they arrested 68 Wolves' fans, which included blokes I went with and knew well. Fellas like Richie Wright, Wayne Parry, Chrissey Wright, Howey, Kingsley, Gary Painton, Steve Hackett, Alan Spears, Steve Preston, and Pete Whitter. We were known at the time as the "Bridge Boys". I think Kingsley was the one that came up with the name but I don't know where he got it. It was rumoured that the Old Bill took over a year to come up with that title for this operation. We weren't the first mob to be dawn raided. Chelsea and West Ham had been involved in their own police operations with operations "Own Goal" and "Full Time". Even the smaller clubs such as Crystal Palace were shown on prime time T.V. having their front doors removed by burly arsed policemen, but like most good things they have to sadly come to an end and nearly all these police football gang show trials, which are normally associated with Third World countries, collapsed. The police even held their own inquiries into these stage-managed, dawn raids. Still, the compensation paid out by the police and the authorities for wrongful arrest, and in some cases imprisonment for police dodgy evidence, has left some of those incarcerated laughing their bollocks off. Some now run successful businesses with their compensation payouts and I should know. I've even drunk in a couple of their bars out in Thailand. With our operation, they planted two undercover police officers in with our lot and we didn't have a clue they were there. Part of their evidence was a video they'd shot at an away game at Scarborough. It showed one of our lads, Carlton, who weighed about twenty stone, sitting on a fence and bouncing up and down as he tried to break it in half. They'd been following us and filming us and gathering evidence for eighteen months. The gang we'd started had just kept on getting bigger and bigger and it had a snowball effect. The more bother we got into the bigger the "Bridge Boys" numbers grew. We did become massive and I suppose that's what drew the police's interest in us. The 68 arrested were interviewed at various police stations in the Wolverhampton area. Some were held in Red Lion Street, some in Wednesfield and others at Brierley Hill. I sat in the cell in the police station and knew I was in some serious shit. I thought I'd fucked my life up for good and couldn't believe what a silly cunt I'd been. I had a nice bird that loved me, our own place even though I had to pay half the bills, but I was still madly in love with her. I was remanded in custody at a place for under twenty one year olds, called Brockhill Hill, Reditch. It's now a women's prison. I'd been arrested at home, questioned at the police station, taken to court and remanded, all on the same day. My brief, who was called Andrew Brocklehurst, who's now a good pal of mine, tried his hardest to keep me out of jail but the prosecution wanted me remanded to keep me, they said, from interfering with witnesses. I'd been charged at the Old Bill station with conspiracy to violent disorder, unlawful violence and conspiracy to burgle a jeweller's shop in Wolverhampton. They were all conspiracy charges, Gary Painton, and me were banged up together and the rest, who were over 21, were sent to Winston Green. I'm not frightened or embarrassed to admit it, but the first night on remand I was physically ill. Because it was late in the day we were taken to prison by police car. I was placed in a cell on my own on the hospital wing, I was given a brown prison jacket and trousers and blue and white striped shirt and I was given a meal of Beef Stroganoff which didn't have a lot of meat in it. I was banged up straight away but it wasn't long before I sicked the whole lot of the meal up. It went everywhere, all over the bed and on the floor. It stank. The next morning a screw called the doctor in to have a look at me but he just put the sickness down to nerves and not having been to prison before. I was as white as a sheet and shaking like fuck.

After four days I was placed in a dormitory with a T.V. and it soon became clear that some of the people in there should not have been in there at all. There was some real sad cases banged up who were mentally ill and really should have instead been in a psychiatric hospital and not locked up in prison. I was half lucky and got out after ten days but poor old Gary was banged up for a further fifteen months. How the fucks do people who are sentenced to long terms inside handle it? When I got home, my girlfriend could not cope with it as it had all got too much for her, I could see the pain, and hurt I had put her through. She used to just sit there in floods of tears and eventually it split us up. I couldn't blame her as she was only young and deserved someone better than me.

When my case came to court. I only had the two violent disorders to face as the rest of the charges were dropped. I was found guilty and given two hundred and eighty hours community service. Result! Some of the other lads didn't fare so well. It was just before Christmas and Howey got fifteen months and Kingsley got twenty-one months. It was a big trial that went on for weeks and there was a lot of plea-bargaining going on. Some pleaded guilty and it looked at one point in the trial that the judge might just throw it out of court, but we never had so much luck. All the lot of us were also banned from attending football for the next five years, which at the time was unheard of.

A few of the boys on having football taken out of their lives jumped on the rising rave scene bandwagon. It was 1990 and all that love and peace and Es, and shouts of Acccciiiid did nothing for me. Drinking bottles of water at £10 a time at open air raves and taking ya tops off and dancing bare-chested to a moronic robotic beat while being swathed in strobe lighting, what the fuck was that all about?

I replaced football with a new woman in my life. I'd met a bird in a nightclub in Dudley and within two months, we were living together. Debbie was different from Mandy in lots of ways and for a while, we got on great. She'd already had a son from a previous relationship which to be honest never bothered me. I was settling down nicely away from football when a mate of mine told me that two coach loads of our lot

Me aged 6 with my uncle Gilly

Aged 16, off to an away game. That's not my caravan in the background.

Me at 18 with pal Pete Matthews

My first love,
Mandy

Kev Coats and me on my 21st

Italy 1997 with the boys

Pisa, when we
fucked off without
paying for the meal

The badly built tower
in Pisa

Celebrations with the draw in Italy

The boys in
Italy, showing
the Italians
how to dress

Carl and Bona

Rome – cheerup lads,
say cheese

Me, Preston and
Painton in Rome

Me, Danny and Preston, we fooled the police and flew to Crete

Bona, Bracken and the lads window-shopping in London

were travelling down to London to watch Wolves play at West Ham. "Don't worry about the Old Bill" said the fella, "they've run out of funding to follow us about". I smiled and it certainly gave me food for thought but did I want to go back to my old ways? Only time would tell.

CHAPTER FOUR

THE BOYS ARE BACK IN TOWN

The two packed coaches come to a halt right outside the Boleyn Pub, which is on the junction of Barking Road and Green Street a few locals peered out of the windows but by the looks of it West Hams boys had long gone, we all piled off and into a back street pub just around the corner from the ground. There was no Old Bill about to meet and greet us and the streets were deserted. The game had already started and we were looking for some action. A few of the boys hung about outside the pub chatting with drinks in their hands, a few others had gone off scouting and the rest are at the bar chucking beer down their necks. There were no West Ham fans in the pub but at the top of the street, you could see the odd one or two of their boys walking past and clocking what we were up to. After about twenty minutes, a mob of about 40 or 50 of them appeared at the top of the road some were dressed in tee shirts or Hawaiian shirts and shorts. It's a warm, sunny day and this West Ham mob looked like they've time-share boys from Tenerife. The pub empties and we walk slowly towards them. It's game on and there's not a copper in sight. I'm still humming Adamski and Seal's hit, "Killer". As I strolled towards them, I must have heard it ten times on the pub's jukebox, and it drives ya mad, as it's one of them songs you can't get out of your head. It goes toe-to-toe with this West Ham firm, who are as game as fuck and don't budge an inch. Passers by are joining in and I even see a geezer get out the front passenger seat of a car, hand the woman next to him the baby he's had on his lap, and come steaming into us. "Come on you cunts" he shouts. Slowly we start to get the upper hand and with sheer weight of numbers we start to back their boys up and it's stop start, stop start as the fighting carries on all the way up towards Plaistow. We reach an off-licence and a few more locals join in. If they'd had a few more boy's we could have quite easily come unstuck. They were as game as fuck. The Old Bill arrives and splits the two groups. The Old Bill gets us; onto the underground and escorts, us on the tube back to Euston Station. I look around as we were being put on a main line train back to Birmingham. It seemed that our lot were back together again but this was the last game of the season. Would everyone be so keen for the start of the next season or was this just a one off?

During the summer months, I found plenty to do. I kept in touch with the boys from football and at weekends we'd meet up and have a few beers and talk about the forthcoming season and what it held in store, both on and off the pitch. We were once regarded as a big club but for a good few years now we'd been languishing around in the lower leagues not really doing anything.

At home in Debbie's flat on the Rocket- pool Estate which is in Bradley near Bilston, all was well. We were getting on just fine and Ricky, her baby son from another bloke, was growing up quickly and things had progressed on after our first date when I took her to the pictures where we saw "Buster" the story of Buster Edwards and the great train robbery. She wanted to go and see the big blockbuster of the time, which was "Pretty Woman" starring Julia Roberts and Richard Gere, or even worse, she wanted to see "Ghost" with Patrick Swayzee and Demi Moore. I didn't fancy sitting up the back row with her crying into a Kleenex while I had the popcorn. She ribbed me for months afterwards about my choice of film for a first date but it was water off a duck's back. Debbie was a good looking girl with a lovely figure who was a great cook and kept a nice, clean home. She came from Tipton where the legendary Wolves hero Steve Bull came from and most of the local population speak Chinese, well it sounds like it anyway. "Wheel yowl breeng in the whushing" or "eye hay" would translate as "Will you bring in the washing" and "eye hay" is "I aint". Theirs is a real Black Country accent. I know the people from Wolverhampton and the surrounding areas get some stick about the way we talk and we get called Yam Yams because we say things like "where am ya?" for "where are you?" or "yam a wanker" for "you're a wanker". Yam is really "you" or "you're", but then just up the road you've got the more nasal sound of a Brummie accent, which sounds like someone bunged up with a head cold or more likely Columbian Flu. According to most Southerners and Scousers, Jocks and Geordies, anyone living between Stoke and just north of Oxford is a Brummie and has more than likely appeared or been an extra in Crossroads. Anyway, Debbie's family were the salt of the earth with both her Dad and older brother Mark, Wolves' fans. I wasn't keen on her mum though. I think she thought I wasn't good enough for her daughter but as a young couple, we found plenty of things to do together and from what I can remember it was mostly shagging. We were at it like rabbits. Well you do when you first get together but sadly, the novelty soon wears off having the old Jack and Danny on tap so to speak.

May soon came which saw the start of Italia 90. I didn't get to go out there but here is my mate Abbos account of went on. Saturday, 2nd June 1990, we're sitting in our local pub and England are playing a pre World Cup friendly against Tunisia with added interest for us because Wolves player, Steve Bull, is in the squad. England are losing 1-0 and Bull pops up and gets an equaliser. Should we or shouldn't we go? Ah fuck it let's go. Therefore, Wednesday it's down to the passport office in Peterborough for a ten-year passport. Thursday, book a flight from Heathrow to Rome and then on to Calagari, Sardinia. We hadn't even checked in at Heathrow and the Met spot us, give us a pull so that was that. On the plane a bag of clothes, a pocket full of money, no accommodation, no tickets and no fucking idea what we were doing.

We land in Rome where it's hot and smoggy, and with two hours to kill before our connection, we head for the bar. Two lagers 5 quid. Looking around we're surprised to see not many English about. Then a couple of lads come over, one Watford, one Chelsea, so we had a few beers and tried to pick their brains to see where they were staying and where they were going, but they appeared to be as lost as us. So we caught the connecting flight to Sardinia and landed late at night and headed for the train station in the middle of the city. Sardinia didn't know what the fuck was about to hit it. Everywhere was shut and there was a few English milling around. We waited on the station until it got light and went out the side door to have a look in the street. We got chatting to three lads from Bristol, one lad from Millwall and a Yid. It seemed like a lot of people were going to camp. Apparently there were two campsites, one official and another unofficial. After another ten minutes of talking this through we went up a side street, bought a tent, hopped in their van, and drove to the campsite. On the way down it worked out that Wilf, Rob and Ian, the Bristol lads, had driven down and picked up Millwall Dave and Dick the Yid, on the way. As we drove down the main road we took a left down a country lane, which subsequently led to a beach road. On the right was our campsite and on the left was a five star hotel so we went in, paid our fees, pitched our tent andgot on the piss. That night we went into the local town, Pula. This was also where the England training camp was based. After getting our bearings we made our way to the bar. The bar was open air and there was quite a few lads sitting around the tables having a beer. QPR, Chelsea, Southampton, and a few lads from Walsall. We stayed and had a few beers.

Had a morning on the beach, got back into the campsite and the FSA had bought down crossword books and pens and a fucking video jukebox. They thought this was going to stop any trouble, but within a few hours of this the freak show had started. A couple of lads were walking down the road when a car full of Italians pulled up. After a few words a fight breaks out and one of the English lads is stabbed. A short while later a few more locals turn up in cars and drive along the beach road towards the campsites but in the tiny road the cars can't turn around so the Italians then find themselves stuck between two mobs of English, one from each campsite. The cars get wrecked and the Italians get slapped. But within twenty minutes two coaches of Carabineri, all kitted out in rull riot gear, surround the campsite and put on a bit of a show of strength. After a short stand-off there were no arrests that night.

The next day England were training so we drove up to the training ground in the Bristol lad's van. Got to the training ground, had a few snaps taken with the England players, Gazza, Neil Webb, Peter

Beardsley, Terry Butcher, and had a real good crack with them. Next thing on the agenda was to find match tickets so we returned to the railway station. It didn't take long to find an Italian who appeared to have more tickets than the English F.A. We bought three, all at face value. After that we got back to the campsite and were met by Billy from Arsenal, who was as paranoid as fuck of everyone being undercover Old Bill. But to be honest I didn't give a fuck. It was my first touring duty with England and I was having a blast. The night bought a tour of the local town. The Italians were playing and they had got a big screen in the town centre. The locals had gathered, not only to watch the game but to watch the circus, but unfortunately for them after a bit of bottle throwing and the usual abuse of the Old Bill, there were no problems at the end.

The next day is the day of the Ireland game. They were based in Corsica or Sicily and obviously at this time it was the height of the troubles in Northern Ireland so we knew that the bomb chuckers were coming in by ferry which was located half way between the railway station and the ground. Ambush! Fucking joking. More Old Bill than Paddies, so after passing through all the security checks we finally enter the ground. A brand new, open-air stadium with twelve foot Perspex fence around the perimeter, followed by a moat, followed by heavily armed police officers. The match finished one each, what a load of bollocks. Everybody is in high spirits but no Paddies to fight, so people begin to squabble between themselves. After walking back to the town, we have a few beers and some verbal exchanges with the locals and everyone returns back to the campsite for some late night drinking in our bar. It was hard to stay in the tents because during the day the temperatures rose to over 100 degrees, so it was up and shower then back to the bar. Kenny (QPR), Billy (Arsenal), and Charlie (Chelsea), were already on the piss with big chunks of black on the table so you just rolled your own. By mid-afternoon everybody was pissed and stoned and people began to tell stories of other England tours. I am sitting there with some of England's finest lads knowing that back home the lads would be jealous as fuck. Reports of skirmishes from the previous night had filtered back to the site as different people had bumped into other people in the town. The official campsite next to ours seemed to be getting a lot more police attention than ours did. Plain-clothes snatch squads had grabbed a few and arrested them after trouble in the town the previous night.

The next couple of days were spent killing time as the Dutch game loomed. We trekked around the island with the Bristol lads, Dave and Rich, which bought us to the night before the Dutch game when one of the scariest moments I have ever witnessed in twenty-five years of following football unfolded in front of me. The usual suspects are pissed and stoned in the camp bar. It is dusk. Two middle-aged, smartly dressed Italians are standing at the bar talking to the geezer behind the counter. The shorter of the two men clocks a chunk of black on the table. Speaking no English, he tries to tell us that what is being smoked is illegal. He is told to get fucked when the next thing that comes out is his warrant card. He is fucking Old Bill. In a flash, over comes a plastic chair followed by a bottle, and then out comes his gun. Fuck that. I'm on the floor and then I hear cries of "get him, get him". The officer backs off waving his gun as bottles and glasses shower him. His mate then joins him and they cower off around the corner into the road. We all pile onto the road. Crack, crack, crack. I'm back on the floor. Looking up, fifteen or so lads are chasing them into the beach road. More bottles and glasses smash onto the road. Crack, crack, two more shots. The two officers then run towards the five star hotel on the beach screaming to the security guards to open the gates, and in they go. Fuck me, my heart was pounding and the adrenalin was pumping. Everybody looks at each other and everybody starts laughing. A couple of lads off the site are having a meal in the hotel when the two Old Bill come flying through the restaurant doors. One still has the gun in his hand, puts it on the counter, and is screaming in Italian to the manager. He gives him the phone. Fifteen minutes later six cars of police and two coaches of Carabineri turn up at the campsite gates. These mean business. Full riot gear, batons, rifles and tear gas canisters. Everyone is back in their tents looking through gaps, watching robocops drag people out of their tents and basically rough them up. We just sat in the tent hoping that the next people they dragged out weren't going to be us. But after an hour it all calmed down so we went out and about and over to the Bristol tent, where we had a chat about a mad night.

The next morning is the day of the Dutch game. As with the Irish, they were based on another island and were coming in by ferry, but this time we were going to get into the bars that lined the route to the ground. We got into the town and the amount of English had seemed to double from the Irish game. There were a lot of well-known English faces about. After a couple of hours in the bars, the ferry pulls in. How many Dutch? How game? Doesn't really matter as England have a quality mob out. These were the days before replica shirts and painted faces. The majority of people here were up for it. Now we just had to sit and wait for the Dutch to come off the ferry. Pouring off, they came in a sea of orange. Wigs, boiler suits and plastic boobs. Not a lad in sight. How can you hit these people, what a let down? The Old Bill and the press get their way anyway. The Old Bill get heavy handed with a mob of English who have started to throw bottles into the Dutch escort on the opposite side of the street. Batons and rifle butts connect with the heads and faces of the unfortunate few that get caught in the street, and the odd waft of tear gas drifts our way. It is time to get out the way and we go, through the checkpoint and all the searches as usual, to the ground. The atmosphere in the stadium with no roof is as good as it gets. Hundreds of flags and thousands of English, but the game is an anti-climax, nil – nil, a bit like the Dutch firm, but in 1993 we get a chance to put it right.

Next day we take a trip to the local supermarket to replenish the supplies of German lager and cheap Italian plonk. A quiet day roaming the site and chatting to everybody to see what their view of last night's fiasco was. The Bristol lads had decided to cook a meal for a few of us that night. After a few lagers I decided to get a few bottles of wine out and I asked for a bottle opener. Wilf said that it was in the black bag inside the door, and whilst looking around in the bag I spot a little tag inside which reads Avon and Bristol Constabulary. Fuck me, Old Bill. I call over my brother and Dicky for a second and third opinion. Fuck me, undercover Old Bill, so it's one of the Bristol lads. Wilf, 6'4", twenty stone? Rob, covered in tattoos? Ian, on the front of steaming it? But I had seen them all smoke drugs. Maybe the paranoia of the Londoners could be true. Do we mention it to anybody else on the site? These people had driven us all over Sardinia, cooked for us, drunk with us. What a situation. After more booze and drugs my bottle went anyway and we never asked them.

So the next day the three of us schemed and planned how to work out who was Old Bill. Looking around the site it looked like a few people had left after the Dutch game, and the Egypt game was a couple of days away. Nobody seemed to be bothered and everything was subdued. A few more reports of arrests and deportations and of sporadic assaults by the Italian police and locals were doing the campsite grapevine. But our dilemma did not go away. Even me finding three hundred pound rolling down the beach road didn't help.

Egypt, the final game, was upon us. Very few Egyptians had made the journey but a couple of Egyptian naval ships had docked in the port and the men were in full uniform with a marching band. But we needed to win to get onto the mainland and the numbers of English had dwindled away. A 1-0 victory was enough.

The night passed off pretty peacefully with no reports of any arrests or madness in the town, so it was back down the campsite for a few beers. Millwall Dave had gone to bed. Me and Dick and the three Bristol lads were around the table. "Well, who is Old Bill then?" I have never sobered up so quick. These were off to the mainland tomorrow and we were off home Saturday, so now seemed the right time. The three lads looked at each other and Ian said "it's me, what you gonna do"? "Fuck all" I said. He then went on to explain to us that he was Old Bill. He wasn't under cover, he just loved his football. I know you say you can never trust a copper, but I ended up travelling with him to Euro 92 and even went down to Bristol with him for a beer on a few occasions and he was never under cover. But what a story and what a buzz. Telling people that you travelled and fought with an English copper. So we said our goodbyes and they went on to Riminey. On the Saturday we left a virtually empty campsite to fly home and we vowed to return to the semi-final and final, but work and money didn't let this happen. Euro 92 would be a different story though. I would be wiser and better prepared.

June's the month when all that's on T.V in the way of sport is the Derby from Epsom or fucking boring Wimbledon tennis it aint so bad if there's a couple of good sorts playing and you get to see a bit of snatch or a glimpse of their tits. The end of July sees the start of footballs' pre-season friendlies when teams from the football league go around playing teams from non-league football. You'd play someone like Sutton United or Cannock Rangers or Aldershot on a Friday night, you'd travel down there, and the team would be made up of youth or reserve team players. A total waste of time them pre-season friendlies although one pre-season we did play Chelsea at the Molineux and nearly 7,000 turned out as we drew 2-2 with Chelsea's first team but there was no reports of any trouble. August would see the start of the football season kick off with the Charity Shield at Wembley a game usually between the League champions and the F.A. Cup winners. It always seemed to be Arsenal and Man. Utd. contesting this game, probably because they have been the two most successful sides over the last fifteen years, except for the year when they both had a blip and Blackburn paid huge amounts of money to loan the title for a year. Our own Chairman at Wolves, Sir Jack Hayward, was never frightened to dip into his own pocket to fund the club in the transfer market or for ground improvements. However, the late Sir Jack Walker a local Blackburn businessman and big time fan spent millions and millions on the likes of Alan Shearer, Chris Sutton, David Batty, Tim Sherwood, all expensively assembled by Kenny Dalglish and Ray Harford, and because of that have always been accused of buying the Premiership Crown. But I believe that was just sour grapes look at the money Arsenal and United have spent on players over the years and that was when almost all the other clubs were skint no I say good luck to Blackburn.

It was around the end of July – August when Debbie broke the news to me that she was pregnant and was expecting our first baby. It didn't come as a shock; after all we'd put in a fair bit of practice!

Wolves kicked off the season with a home defeat to Oldham Athletic losing 3-2, Steve Bull getting two for us in front of a crowd of just over 21,000 which wasn't bad for a second division game. We then played Port Vale away and won 2-1 and we had our customary scrap with the locals from Burslem. The Port Vale Beer Monsters always turn out for a big game at home but don't travel too well, unlike their close neighbours Stoke City, who we've had some right battles with over the years.

This season saw us play our nearest rivals, West Bromwich Albion, something that hadn't happened for a few years. Although a lot of us were still on banning orders, we were still allowed outside the stadiums but risked arrest if caught inside a ground. About fifteen of us had just had a good row with a West Brom. firm on the corner of Halfords Lane and Birmingham Road. In their mob was Joey Clarke and Chrissey Lewis two of their black lads who are as game as fuck and two people who I have the greatest respect for. The Old Bill turned up and pushed us back up onto a concrete ramp just outside the ground. They surround us and then informed us that we were all being arrested for breaking our banning orders. We all looked at one another. "You are on the property of West Bromwich Albion Football Club," they said. We've been set up big time. We were arrested, charged and taken to court and each given a £200 fine. At the home game, the Baggies (West Brom.) turn up about 60 handed and they were immediately surrounded by the Old Bill. We had a massive mob of about 700 waiting for them out on the streets. We couldn't get anywhere near them and were driven back by the Old Bill into the town centre. Scuffles broke out with the police, which soon turned into running battles with shop windows getting smashed after the game the Albion fans were held back inside Molineux and then escorted to safety. Over the years, the biggest mob they've ever come to our place with is about 100 but they've never done anything, but when we play them at the Hawthorns we always go there in big numbers and go looking for it. That's the difference between the two sets of fans.

Another Midlands' team that I've rated up until recently is Leicester. Now I don't rate them at all but in the 80s and 90s you were guaranteed a row at Filbert Street and a couple of times we've been over there we've clashed with them near the prison. The game I remember was a night game and 60 to 70 of us arrived late and were having a look around it was dark and to tell you the truth we didn't see them coming. There were fucking hundreds of them; they were like ants crawling all over us. We came right unstuck and got run in every direction, totally outnumbered and fucked. After the game, we met up with the rest of our boys who'd been in watching the game, and we then gave a much better account of ourselves.

The 90/91 season saw us play teams with good mobs. Barnsley turned up about 60 handed and even drank in one of our main pubs. They were big, strapping coal mining types who were as game as fuck. They caught about six of us and I was kicked to fuck. Pompey came in a big, well-dressed mob and looked impressive. They were well up for it and were one of the biggest firms I'd ever seen at Wolves. Over the years when we've played them, they've always turned out, a top firm. Newcastle is another mental mob, not so much interested in being fashion conscious but just up for it. They turn up in their black and white striped shirts and I've even seen a couple of their fans in kilts.

Plymouth have also turned out both home and away when we've played them and over the years the two sets of fans have had the utmost respect for one another. A few of their boys and our lot get together at England games. Millwall that particular season were a major disappointment and turned up about 25 handed. They were a very young lot and got run all over the place before the game. They were living on a past reputation. I know that Millwall have nearly always had a top firm and anyone who says they don't rate them is an idiot. However, on this day they came unstuck but they got their revenge a few years later when they turned up in a night game, 300 strong, and cut one of our lot down the face with a blade.

Sheffield Wednesday were another club with a big reputation and we'd heard they'd taken 250 boys to Bristol Rovers that season, but they failed to show up at our place. They're a bit like the other Sheffield side, United, who pick their away games carefully. I've heard about them and their B.B.C. (Blades Business Crew) going here, there and everywhere and running this mob and 500 of them running so and so, but they again never really showed up at Molineux. The same could be said of West Ham. We'd had a blinding row with them at the end of the previous season but a couple of times we didn't travel to them and they didn't come to us. Too many Es, eh? AAAAAACCCCCIIIIIIIIIIIIIDDDDDD.

That season in the League Cup, we played Hull City. We drew 0-0 up there and was expecting a massive turn out from them in the 2nd leg their firm had a big reputation but it was a disappointing night all round as we went out after drawing 1-1 after extra time and their boys failed to show up. The season before in the same competition, we'd beaten Lincoln City over two legs and then drew Aston Villa in the next round. The first leg was at Villa Park and the majority of fans in the 27,000 crowd sounded like they were Wolves fans. We lost 2-1 but had been optimistic of turning it around in the 2nd leg, and maybe even going all the way to the final of a competition we'd won twice before in 1974 and 1980. The return leg was in early October and before the game, there was no sign of the promised Villa mob. They'd told a few of our boys at the game a few weeks before that they'd be putting on a show over at our place. About seventy of us were standing on the grass bank above the subway where the Wolves' Subway Army years before had earned its reputation and had gotten their name from. They used to ambush visiting fans in the underpass which connected the town centre to the football stadium and from which you could see part of the pitch and a little of the on-field action. "Who's that lot?" said one of our boys shouting and pointing into the dark shadowy distance. In the blackness you could just make out a crowd of moving heads with just the orange glow of the street lamps illuminating their purposeful movement. We moved off towards them and as we fanned out across the tarmac there stood was less than a hundred yards between us and them, as we got closer we could see they were a mob of strangers. There were no familiar, friendly faces in amongst this lot. I was at the front and now there was less than twenty yards between us and them we walked slowly and purposefully towards them, we were going nowhere running was'nt an option that thought would not have entered our heads. They had now decided to stop and were bouncing up and down with their arms waving up and down like swans. Not a good sign it looks as though they were'nt to sure. A few looked behind them, again not a good sign, then their front line parted and a bloke from their rear stepped forward and threw a smoking canister into us."C Crew. C Crew" they chanted I coughed and spluttered as tears streamed down my cheeks. I wiped my eyes and cracked one of them on the jaw. That was the signal for them to turn and run but for a few moments it looked like there was going to be a good row on the cards with no Old Bill and even numbers it could have been a blinder, but as quickly as they'd appeared they as quickly disappeared.

Over the years when we've played Villa we've always seemed to have got the upper hand but in the last few years they've got a good, solid, hard-core firm together with Fowler, Tucker and Steely some of their top faces.

December saw the team languishing near the bottom of the division and it, also saw the birth of my son. He weighed in at 7lb 11ozs and I was present at his birth at New Cross Hospital, Wolverhampton. He was a ringer for my mum an absolute double who, along with my Nan, was as proud as punch. "You've made your bed me lad, now lie on it" said mum. I spent the next two days at home looking after young Ricky who was now nearly two years old. This might just be the event that could change my ways and settle me down into becoming a loving family unit. After two days in hospital, Debbie came home with the new arrival, Adam Gilroy Shaw. She's always claimed that she chose the name but I chose his name, hence his middle name of Gilroy. The song playing on the radio as we drove back home from the hospital was The Farm and "Altogether Now". I always remember that song and the video that went with it. I think places and times and songs and where you are and who you are with always seem to stick in peoples' minds. Well they do mine anyway.

I'm not sure if it was the 1991-1992 season but it was around that time when we played Peterborough away and I travelled there with me mate in his car. It's only about an hour and a quarter drive from Wolverhampton so I knew our lot would travel there in big numbers. We all met in a pub before the game and about 10 of us made our way to the ground and went in the home end. The seats and the terraces began to fill up just before kick-off, and there seemed to be a mob of Wolves in all parts of the ground. A fight started in the seats on the sideline and fans were scattering everywhere to get out of the way. One of their lot, a big, black lad, is taking a right battering and is thrown head first from the upper section into the fans in the seats below. We jumped onto the pitch from behind the goal and joined in and then the Old Bill came in and broke it up, and restored order. After the ref blows for full time there's scuffles and fighting out in the streets and a mob of our lot attack a snooker hall were a load of black kids and Rastas come steaming out at them, the locals are chased back inside and the windows go in and the place is wrecked. At the end of that season, we lost our last two games against Barnsley and Boro and finished 11th in Division 2. The European championships out in Sweden kicked off in June I didn't go because of one thing and another but Abbos brother Carl and a few of our lads made the trip. Here in Carls own words is what went on.

Sweden 92. I was excited as this was to be my first England trip abroad. I went with my brothers and a couple of other lads. We had a minibus and drove across Europe. We stayed at the unofficial campsite in Malmo, in a big house tent.

We went to Malmo Square where the Battle of Malmo took place. They had a big beer tent; you know the kind, a big, marquee type. Some lads were drunk and were dancing on the roof and the police didn't really know what to do. They managed to get them down but were a bit heavy-handed in doing so. The mounted police were sent in and England went mad. It was probably the best row I've seen abroad with England. They belted the Old Bill with chairs, tables, bottles and anything else they could get their hands on. It is the only time I have ever seen mounted police do one. They sent in the dog handlers next and the same happened again. Then the riot police came in, and they ran off. The police lost all control for about an hour and the town was looted and trashed. England fans attacked a cameraman. They threw his camera through a window and knocked him out. Another bloke was driving down the street on a motorbike. He was knocked off and his bike was set on fire. One copper got caught and had a right kicking. His colleagues hadn't realised he had been caught at first, but when they did, they came back. Someone had got the copper's hat and baton. Then rumours started to go around that a couple of England fans had been stabbed by local Moroccans and Turks. Clashes and scuffles were going on all across the city. The rumour was that the locals were going to attack the campsite so we all got tooled up and had a bonfire. Someone set the cabins on fire and a load of taxis pulled up. We all went across the field towards the gates. With just their shorts on and bare chests out, the England boys tooled up and approached the taxis, but they didn't have to stand long as the locals fled, and the taxis with them.

The day after was red hot. There was a beach and a nudist beach on the site. All the England boys were milling around with their shades on, and holding cans of beer, and some of the lads were swimming and playing football. So my first couple of games in Malmo had been very eventful.

On to Stockholm, the capital of Sweden. There weren't many places to camp here so they put us in the athletics stadium. All the tents were up and the campfires were going, and so were the beers. Now I don't drink spirits as a rule, but the whisky was flowing that night. My brothers and the others went to bed but 30 or so England boys, including myself, decided to go for a drink down a local beer tent. When we arrived there a scuffle was going on with about 20 English boys and approx. 100 skin-heads, called the Black Army. We ran to help and that made about 50 of us. We gave it to them big time. The Old Bill turned up and a police car was overturned onto its side, and later everyone went back to the campsite. The next morning the Old Bill raided the site and nicked me. I was still pissed. They took me to a police station and I was held there until court, which was 2 days later.

While I was arrested there was a game against Sweden, which England lost. After the game, some of the local fans and the England boys clashed. It was broadcast on television and it showed you some of the locals taking savage beatings. A few more English had been arrested. The next morning I went to court and was remanded. I told my brothers and mates not to wait for me and they left my stuff and went home. I was on a 23-hr lock up with 1-hour exercise on the roof, where you could only see the sky. I had plenty of money on me but the food in there was wank. Thank God for the trolley that came round. The trolley used to stop outside the cells, which they would unlock, so that we could buy from it. It had food, snacks and a well-known newspaper, which I would read. The other lads, who were locked up, wrote their firm's name on the top of the newspaper. There was the 657, the Baby Squad, Suicide Squad, Newcastle, I hadn't realised how many. This was how I met a good and loyal friend called Pot who was from Burnley. We managed to get a cell next to each other and they would open the door in the middle so we could chat and have exercise together.

After a week they would put little televisions in the cell, which had one English Channel, and we would watch old movies or series like Minder. They were only 15 years behind but still; it managed to pass the time away. I got myself a solicitor and told them that my missus was pregnant. I kept going to court and they kept trying to do me for instigating a riot. They were trying to do Pot for the vicious kicking he gave to one of the Swedes outside the ground, and for robbing his watch. We were in and out of court and they kept saying I was from Tottenham, and I kept telling them I was from Wolves. In the end they deported me back to England after spending 30 days on remand. I said my goodbyes to Pot and told him I would stay in touch.

The Old Bill walked me to the plane, handcuffed like I was a terrorist, and off I went home. When I got back I was on the front page of the local paper and the headlines read, "Judge sends hooligan home because girlfriend's expecting". For the first couple of weeks people kept taking the piss and asking me when it was due. So O.K., I told a little, teeny weenie lie, but I was due a bit of luck.

That was my first trip abroad with England but me and the Burnley lad, Pot, stayed mates and have had many battles abroad with England, and you will read in this book about everyone since.

We start the 92-93 season, with a 2-0 away win at Brentford we then beat Leicester at home 3-0 and then go another 11 games before we suffer our first loss of the season 2-0 away at Millwall. Later on my daughter, Demi-Leigh, was born. I remember it clearly we had Tranmere Rovers away and I didn't go to the game as I was at the New Cross Hospital watching her birth. Her name came about as I liked the name Demi and Debbie had a cousin named Jodie-Leigh, so we settled on Demi-leigh. She was a dead ringer for me but then all babies must look like me when they're born! Around this time the rows between Debbie and me started, because she was so jealous of me. She didn't like the fact that I had loads of mates and that I'd often meet up with them. Don't get me wrong, I loved her and the three kids to bits and I didn't ignore them in any way, but she was just so jealous and possessive. It seemed she wanted me just for herself and resented me having friends, and she also now hated me going to football. Well I was going to football but I couldn't get in to watch the games me and the boys would just hang around out-side and that's what she couldn't work out or understand "If you can't go in what's the point in going?" she would ask me. I couldn't answer her, she was right, but going to football with the boys was in my blood. I couldn't explain to her in words why I did what I did. "You're all daft, the lot of ya" she'd say and she was right. But so what? "Grow up" was another one she would come out with.

Many of these smaller clubs in the lower divisions can pull a tidy firm on their day and usually these firms are made up of not just football fans but locals from all walks-of-life and occupations Skinheads, Mods, Bikers, Hells Angels, Asians, and black lads. The whole town will some-times come together and turn out for a row when a team rolls into their town with a bit of a reputation. A few years back Wolves had drawn Wigan in the F.A. Cup. We were a 3rd division team and they were in the 2nd. The train I travelled up there on was banged out with Wolves fans and out of a train load there must have been about 300 boys on there, who were up for it. Police with dogs met us as soon as we pulled into the station and then got us out onto the street, and marched us through the grim, grey streets of Wigan. Each pub and social club we passed attracted groups of the locals who would shout abuse at us and taunt us. " Fuck off ya Brummie cunts" If it wasn't for the Old Bill being there, there would have been murders. On arrival at the ground, we were shoved and manhandled towards the turnstiles but loads of us jumped in without paying. How nobody was seriously hurt, I'll never know. The Old Bill on horseback and with dogs, were determined that no one was going to escape from their cordon as they squeezed and pushed us towards the away - end entrances. Inside we were standing on the terraces behind the goal and their main firm were in the corner right next to us. They scored first and we pushed towards them but the lines of coppers between the two mobs held firm and kept us apart. We then equalised and then almost immediately went 2-1 up. We then added a third and it went fucking mental. It was the first time I'd ever seen police horses standing on the terraces. It was fucking complete madness. We were fighting with the Old Bill, as they struggled to hold back the Wigan mob, it was total chaos. It was just running battles with the police as they tried to keep the two mobs apart, the thing was there was only 6,000 fans in the ground, outside it carried on all the way back to the railway station with their mob coming out of side streets and getting stuck into us. Their fans were well game and most of them were dressers with all the latest gear on, this lot weren't your normal northern scruffy bastards The Old Bill held us back at the train station, and tried their hardest to goad us into a fight. "We're not Lancashire police" a senior copper said, "we're the G.M.P. (Greater Manchester Police) so don't fuck with us". The thing is we just had and we didn't give a fuck. We were a young firm who didn't give a shit for no one.

The next round saw us drawn against Bradford City away. We ran a coach up there and parked up near the ground, 50 of us bowled around the back streets and side streets but never saw a soul who looked as though they fancied a fight. We decided to give up looking for their lot and were just going through the away turnstiles when they landed on us. They came straight into us with fists and boots flying and never budged an inch. They called themselves "The Ointment" and were as game as fuck. "No retreat, no surrender" they chanted as we had our backs to the wall with nowhere to go. The Old Bill tried to break it up but give Bradford their due they came through the Old Bill and straight back into us. They were real geezers, not a young lot, just proper men. Nothing happened inside the ground or outside after the match, but big Fat Carlton was in the chip shop queuing for some grub afterwards when his hunger pangs must have got the better of him, anyway a few of their boys spotted him and chased him out of the shop and up the road. I don't suppose they could miss him really as he must have been about 25 stone at the time.

On the way back we decided to stop off at Derby who had been at home to Chelsea. As we drove towards the town- centre, we stopped at some traffic lights. A group of about 20 lads appeared on the path and began banging on the windows and giving us the wankers sign. The front door of the coach was yanked open and we piled off and that was the signal for them to run, we chased them around the corner, but standing there was a mob of about 250. We stopped dead in our tracks. Oops! We'd been well set up. Half of us ran back to the coach and the rest split up and ran in all directions. It was every man for himself. Those that made it back onto the coach were attacked with bricks and bottles. "Get the Chelsea bastards," one of them shouted. "Fucking hell they think we're Chelsea!" The coach had nearly every window put through as many of our boys cowered on the floor showered in broken glass. They destroyed us big time. Me and Andy Kelly done one and some how managed to get back to Derby railway station unscathed. The Old Bill was all over the place and told us there were no more trains that night. It looked dodgy and we had no way of getting home that is until we got talking to an Aston Villa fan who'd been up to watch them up at Leeds, and decided between us to share a taxi back to Birmingham and that we'd split the cost between the three of us. It had been a long and eventful day, and it wasn't long before me and Andy was well away and fast a kip. When we arrived back in Birmingham there was £40 on the taxi meter. The Villa fan began emptying his pockets. "Give us your share lads," he said. "Get fucked," we both said as we climbed out of the cab and walked off laughing.

"Lads, lads lets talk about this" he said almost pleading and with tears in his eyes. We didn't look back, as we left him to pay the fare.

Cardiff was another firm who turned up massive when we were in the old fourth division. Newport, another South Wales team, would also give you a good row down there and Wrexham once turned up at our place one year 50 handed looking for a row, however Cardiff are the top firm to come out of Wales. A few days before we were due to play them a full-scale riot had erupted in Wolverhampton. A black kid had died while being detained by the police in a shop. He'd suffocated or something. Anyway, his arrest and death led to both black and white kids taking to the streets and wholesale robbing and looting taking place. Quite a few people and police were injured and a few of the football lads got involved. The day we played Cardiff, 200 of them turned up at 11 o'clock in the morning at the train station. Our lot was still in their beds as no one was out and ready for them, the Old Bill quickly seized them and escorted them to the ground. The gates didn't open until around about one o'clock so the coppers just put a ring of men around them to stop them moving. Hundreds of us lot gathered within sight of them but they couldn't get at us and we couldn't get anywhere near them. I'd been to a game with wolves down at Swansea, who are Cardiff's biggest rivals, with Mandy Chapman's Dad so I had to behave myself but I never really saw any trouble, yet you talk to some teams and they rate Swansea as highly as Cardiff and you talk to Swansea fans and they don't rate Cardiff full-stop.

Bolton came that season and we beat them 4-0. I remember one of their boys had a furry, Davey Crockett hat on. Me, Peter Witter and Sean Crozier and a few of the other lads had a blinding row with a mob of theirs. They were all big, strapping men and they called themselves "The Billy Whiz Fan Club." That season, we won the League and got promoted, with hatfuls of goals from Steve Bull and Andy Mutch.

But the one game that sticks in my mind was Northampton Town away. I drove down there with a few mates and went into the White Elephant pub. The pub was full and divided between 50 of our lot and about 50 local Rastafarians. These weren't football lads and something just sparked an almighty row, as it kicked off someone threw a glass and it smashed on the table I was standing near. A shard of glass flew up and imbedded itself into my leg, causing a four inch gash which was pissing blood, and it didn't take long before the left leg of my once-blue jeans were crimson. I managed to hobble away and got myself outside and lent up against the wall, a car with an old couple inside slowed down to have a look at what was going on, they could see I was injured and stopped. The fight was still going on as they helped me into the car and drove me down to the local hospital. I waited in A and E for nearly an hour before I was seen by a nurse who pulled a fair sized bit of piece of glass out of my leg and stitched me up. I then I discharged myself and caught a taxi back to the ground, arriving halfway through the match. Has we drove home afterwards we passed the railway station and there was our lot battling with more locals. I don't think they'll forget Wolves in a hurry, but give 'em credit, like many little teams; they turn out and make a show.

CHAPTER FIVE

ENGLAND AWAY

A few of my mates were right into following the England team and I'd been told by them that following the national team was much more fun than watching club football. I'd never been down to Wembley for any game so I even surprised myself when I agreed to go with the boys. My ban didn't cover international games so I was all right to travel.

England was playing in a World Cup qualifier against Holland in Rotterdam and two days before the game me and Gary Painton flew out from East Midlands Airport to Amsterdam. For a while it looked like we were the only England fans out there but then we bumped into some Mansfield Town lads, who were stopping in our hotel, which made me feel a bit better, although we still didn't have a match ticket. The Mansfield boys were proper nice fellas and we were joined by some Blackpool lads. Things were looking up. Pompey turned up in huge numbers and had a right tight firm. Rumours went around that Ajax would be about, but they never showed.

As the day wore on our numbers swelled and a few well-known faces from Chelsea turned up with a few Q.P.R. lads. Oldham's firm swelled our numbers further and we all drank in a bar near to the Red Light district. We were meant to meet in another bar further up the road but the Dutch police heard about it and wouldn't let the bar owner open. I bet he was furious; imagine how much he would have earned with hundred of Englishmen supping his stocks of beer and spirits dry. I should think he had the right hump. He would have suffered a few broken glasses and a bit of boisterous behaviour in exchange for a fistful of guilders. Abbo and Timmy Jay, Brendon Kelly, Indian Joey and the rest of the Wolves lads turned up on the day of the game. Me, and Spats, another well-known Wolves face, travelled down by train to Rotterdam with about 300 other English in a mob. One of Chelsea's main lads seemed to be pulling the strings and running the show. As we pulled into the station where the Rotterdam stadium is we were met by the Dutch Old Bill. We took no notice and walked straight through them as if they weren't there and we were now out on the street on our own with a few coppers bringing up the rear. We couldn't believe it, we were all expecting to be given a hard time but I think we'd caught the Old Bill unaware. It was still only mid-morning and I think they didn't expect us to arrive so early and that must have been the case with the Dutch firm. They must have been at home having their breakfast- time smoke and a pancake or having an early lunch of French fries and mayonnaise. Fuck me, they eat some shit them Dutch. The British have always been accused of having and eating a bland boring diet but the Dutch beat us. You can buy chips smothered in mayonnaise from vending machines and they eat that sort of crispy sausage thing, frigan das or whatever it's called. I've met Dutch people before while on holiday out in Crete who would drive miles to find and eat these things and they look and taste just like shit. Give me roast beef or roast lamb and veg any day. Come to that give me a nice baked hedgehog or a squirrel burger, now we're talking proper grub.

The mob I was with found a square with bars and restaurants surrounding it and settled down outside and had a drink and come mid-day almost every bar was heaving with England fans. The Dutch Old Bill stood out of the way but were watching our every move from a distance.

A few of the lads had England tops on but the majority of the chaps were done up in the latest designer gear. I noticed a couple of the Chelsea lads had tops on with a little green, black and yellow badge on the left arm held on by two little black buttons and from a distance it looked like the national flag of South Africa. However, on closer inspection it looked like the face of a compass with the words "Stone

Island" written on it. I was intrigued and asked one of the cockney lads where he'd got his jumper from. "300 notes this jumper bruv" he grinned as he showed me his gold front tooth. I laughed to myself as I left one of the Mitchell brothers basking in the fact he'd given one of us thick Northerners a tip on what's in and what's out in the world of fashion. For the past few years, Ralph Lauren had been big in the world of terrace fashion and no self-respecting hooligan would dare not to be seen without a little motif on his shirt of a man on horseback swinging a polo stick in mid-air. There was a dress code to be adhered to, a Ralph Lauren jacket or jumper and shirt, Armani or Boss jeans with Timberland boots on your feet. Things had moved on from the days of "phase two" 80s skinheads with their green or blue nylon flight jackets with the bright orange lining. The early 90s was all about style and dressing with a touch of class. You had to wear the labels and if you didn't have the gear, you weren't one of the chaps. It didn't matter if you couldn't fight, it was all about looking the part and oh! Yeah, having a gold tooth took you up another notch.

By early afternoon there must have been well over a thousand strong mob drinking in the square. A small group of Dutch youths appeared at one end, dressed in shell suits, they had long hair and some had pony-tails a few wore baseball caps on back to front. Now the Dutch really don't know how to dress. I didn't expect them to turn up holding a bunch of tulips and with clogs on their feet, but for a nation of hooligans that try to base themselves on the English hooligan culture, they don't have a fucking clue. One of these clowns dressed in a bright orange tracksuit, hurls a homemade nail bomb into a group of English drinking outside a bar. It looked like an armless tennis ball but when it landed, it went off with a real bang. Everyone comes together as the scruffy Dutch run off and the Old Bill move in quickly. Using their batons, they empty all the bars and push everyone down into the next square where they surround us and try to split us up into small groups and put us on board waiting buses. They got rid of most of us but by the last 200 or so they found that they'd ran out of transport so to our surprise they just let us go and we were free to roam. The ones taken away by bus were held in a special camp where, if you had a match ticket, you were released. Those without tickets were held until after the game and in some cases, until the following morning. So much for a free Europe! The mob I was with headed back towards the train station, closely followed by English spotters (Old Bill in plain clothes). You can tell them a mile off with their green wax jackets and brown suede Hush Puppies. They stick out like sore thumbs, as they are too well groomed with their immaculately trimmed moustaches and stinking of Brute aftershave.

As we approached the station, another mob of English came off an inbound train and came bursting out onto the street. I reckon that day we must have had a mob of 5,000 out there. We were awesome, we moved off and as we turned the corner, there were a Dutch firm in front of us. They fanned out across the road and walked towards us. There was about 300 of them, and with no Old Bill in tow, it was game on. I was on the footpath with a Pompey geezer standing next to me when a Dutch geezer whips a metal bike chain out from inside his coat and comes at me, waving it around like Kung-Fu-Nonchacs. "Come on you prick" I shout as I hold my hands up and move towards him I can hear the swish of the chain as he waves it around in the air. The Pompey bloke undoes his three quarter length Aquascutum mac and pulls out an axe. "Come on let's play," he says. "Go on son" I shout excitedly. The Dutchman drops his chain and runs and that's the signal for the lot of them to run. As we chase them up the road another mob of England come out of a side road. At the front are two of the Wolves lot, Spats and Lawley. "Stop them cunts" I shout, and they join in the chase. We catch about 20 of them and they get a bit of a kicking. On the walk back as we grouped up again, I found a flag of Ultrec, which is a Dutch football club, lying in the kerb. That surprised me as I thought that most of the Dutch firm would be from the local team, Feyenoord. For a while things quietened down until a huge mob of English made their way towards the ground just before kick-off. A few Plymouth lads reported back, that they'd seen a mob of Dutch hanging around the stadium so we walked around the ground and near on straight away we bumped into them. A roar went up and we steamed straight in. A few of their frontline pulled blades out and were waving them around and a couple of our lads were slashed before the coppers came wading in, and the Old Bill was well heavy handed. They gave anyone within striking distance a crack over the skull. They were vicious bastards and they scattered us everywhere.

I wound up walking away from the stadium and ended up down back streets with a little mob of 20. A police van drove passed us and stopped 20 yards up ahead. As we approached, the back doors burst open and they jumped out and grabbed the geezer, I'd just moments before been chatting to, they slung him in the back, head first and zoomed off. This geezer was well known on the England scene and was one of Chelsea's main faces. I personally didn't see him again that day but rumour was he'd been taken away and given a beating in the back of the van, justice Dutch style! The Chelsea lads who were with us that knew him blamed the spotters for pointing him out to their Dutch colleagues. Apparently, the English coppers had wanted him for years as he had been a bit of a thorn in their side.

I must admit I did enjoy that trip to Holland and my mates were right, there was far more action following England abroad than watching Wolves. I could definitely get the flavour for it and I'd met up with some good people from other clubs. Yeah, this following England lark was for me.

Back home, it wasn't long before me, Debbie and the kids were on the move and we swapped our flat for a house over in Bradley. The kids loved it as there was more space, with three bedrooms and a front and back garden to play in. Debbie was happier, I was happier, it was all happy families. I decorated the place and for a little while she stopped nagging me but in truth, I couldn't see it lasting.

On the domestic scene one of our lads ran two coaches to Bristol City to see Wolves play down in the West Country. We've never had much to do with either Rovers or City so we weren't on a revenge mission or anything. It was one of the boys' birthdays so we decided to go down there for a day out on the piss more than anything. We stopped in Clifton, just outside Bristol, which is about an hours drive for us. I'd just been given another banning order. I'd finished the last one and within months I was banned again for patting a police horse on the back. As I walked past the horse I patted it on the arse and said "nice horse". This sergeant riding it lent over, grabbed me by the scruff of the neck and ripped my shirt, and pulled me up onto my tiptoes. "You're nicked you prick" he growled into my face, and handed me over to another couple of coppers who were standing near-by. "He's just threatened me" he lied as I was led away. I was charged taken to court where another gavver stood up and lied, saying he'd heard me threaten the cunt on the horse. Again British justice at its best! Guilty until proven guilty and that's why, as a kid, I was told, "Never trust a copper," and the proof was in the pudding.

When we arrived in Clifton the lad whose birthday it was is as pissed as a fart. He falls over, lands in a bush, and rips the arse and the knees out of his trousers. We find a pub while he goes off to a local department store to buy some new strides. He duly buys a new pair of jeans and throws the ripped ones away but as he's that pissed he forgets to check the pockets before slinging them away. Inside is £400, the money he's collected from us for the coach trip.

Mobile phones have now hit the streets and as about 70 of us head for the ground, we get a call from one of the boys who's with about 30 of our lot that have gone for a wander on their own. They tell us they've been attacked by a mob of City and have just been kicked to fuck down near the ground and that the Bristol mob are now in the Hen and Chicken pub. Those who are not banned go into the game and the rest of us, about 20 handed, wander around, looking for the boozer. We cut across a park and stumble across the pub as we approach out they come, throwing bottles and glasses, those that don't smash are picked up by us and hurled back at them. I look around for something to steam into them with and pick up a length of wood and charge into them. I whack the nearest geezer to me over the head and the length of wood disinte-grates into sawdust. The fucking thing was riddled with woodworm! I grab one geezer and was punching fuck out of him when me mate grabs him by the hair and pulls him down, as he does he comes away with a wig in his hand! Well, it was one of the funnies things I'd ever seen. I stopped and was nearly crying with laughter. This bloke shot back into the pub and even his mates tried their hardest not to laugh. How do you ever get over something like that? One minute you're Elvis, with a thick mop of hair then suddenly you're the lead singer from "Right Said Fred". I bet he got some stick later off, of his mates.

The Old Bill rounded us up and slung us into vans, and drove us to a police station on some run-down council estate. The Old Bill only charged Wayne and Mark with a breach of the peace and later let the rest of us go, but because the two coaches which we'd arrived on had gone home already, and because they wanted us out of it, they laid on a coach to take us home.

Me mate Dave had waited outside the police station for me in his car I jumped in and we beat the others home, as we drove through Bristol I laughed to myself at how the local kids were dressed. " East 17" was the big, teeny-bop, chart group of the time and had had a few hit singles plus a number one hit album with "Walthamstow". Their image of baseball caps on back to front or big, woollen, ski hats worn high on their heads, with baggy jeans four or five times larger than required, and plenty of bling bling, was obviously admired by the youths of Bristol. Some of them even had the Staffordshire bull terrier, just like the one the band had used on promotional photos. As we drove out of the city centre and picked up the M5 for home I chuckled to myself. "What's up" asked Dave. "Nothing, I've just got this vision of a bald bloke returning home with a gleaming dome and his wife opening the door to him and letting out a shriek. He'd kept his little secret from her for years and "I bet he never went to work that Monday morning" said Dave.

CHAPTER SIX

THE NAUGHTY FORTY

The Northern Soul Scene 'as always been big business in and around the Potteries, but it's their football mob that is known to most visiting football fans. Go there looking for a row and guaranteed, it won't take long to find it or, more to the point, it won't take them long to find you. For the last four decades Stoke City have had a top mob.

The week before we played Stoke we drew 3-3 with Millwall at home so everyone was out for that game. After the game, Mill wall's mob, were been rounded up by the Old Bill and were put straight on a waiting train back to the smoke. Talk soon got around to the following week's fixture up at Stoke, who over the years we've had some proper good rows with, and, hand on heart, I'd have to say they're the one side that's regularly turned up at The Moline for a row.

About 100 of us had travelled up on the train from Wolverhampton, which is a journey of about forty minutes. A mini-bus and a car full of our lads had left before us and had plotted up in the Phoenix Pub. Apparently their firm were just around the corner in a boozer called The Wheatsheaf. We somehow lost the Old Bill as soon as we arrived and with the boys in the pub we had a good, strong mob of about 100. After a few drinks, our lot start to get a bit bored and restless and want some action. "Drink up" goes the shout, and we pile out into the street where we spread out across the road and go in search of their boys. Turning a corner we literally bump straight into them. It was like one of them old black and white Keystone Cops films where the front ones come to a halt and the back bodies concertina into those in front that have already stopped. This stumbling upon one another looks like it's surprised both firms. The Old Bill come between us before we can clash and push us up a side street, which is set on a bit of a hill. They've been pushed up a road off to the left and we turn and walk off, thinking that's it for the day. We head off up the hill and at the top is a road leading off to the right which leads back down the hill. Their firm as taken their first left which, comes out at the bottom of the hill on which we are standing on the top of. We go bouncing towards them and they do likewise and come up at us. The first geezer within striking distance gets it, with a perfect punch on his chin, and straight away, a copper on horseback chases me through the fighting crowds. Somehow I manage to lose him and get back to the Phoenix Pub where there's still a few of our lads sitting having a pint, oblivious to what's been going on outside. I swap coats with a bloke I know who wasn't involved in the fighting so when a few of our lads get back inside the pub we set off and make our way towards the ground, but as soon as we arrive two Old Bill pull me up and arrest me. Thing is I'd just swapped coats and when I was fighting with their mob I had the hood of the original coat I had on pulled up over my head like a monk. I told the Old Bill they had the wrong man and that I'd not done anything wrong and had only just arrived in town, but "we've seen your face" was all they would say. I was lead away, and charged with violent disorder, assault and possession of a prohibited weapon, which they said was a gas canister, which comes under firearms offences. I told them it was total bollocks and stuck to my story of knowing nothing about a fight between the two mobs. It then got worse as they then claimed that I'd sprayed two policemen with C.S. gas and that I'd been captured on film carrying out this attack. Anyway, I was charged and then while I was in the cell wondering how I was going to get out of this shit, a copper comes in and tells me that I have a phone call from my brother. Well, that puzzled me even further because I aint got a brother. As I was led from the cell down a corridor to an office to take the call, I wondered what these cunts were playing at now.

"Hello Gil" said a voice on the other end of the line. It was Indian Joey. "Alright Bruv?"

"Yea, but these cunts have stitched me right up" I replied, and the copper standing next to me who was listening, smirked.

"Do you want me to come and pick you up when they release you?"

"Where are you?"

"Wolverhampton".

That was Joey for ya, a real friend. The two Old Bill I was meant to have sprayed with gas said they'd suffered with stinging eyes and burning skin on their faces. The fucking liars. There was no gas attack and come to that I'd seen no gas used in the brief fight we'd had. But the police were insistent that they had all this on video and that they would be using it in court as evidence.

When it finally went to court the charges were dropped down to an Affray charge. Also, when the video was shown to the court, my barrister pointed out to the judge and jury that the video showed these two policemen who I have meant to have sprayed with gas, standing in the background, nowhere near where I was. Even on the video, which was of a very poor quality, you couldn't really make out who was who, but you could quite clearly see the two coppers standing perfectly all right in the background. They didn't look like they were suffering the effects of having gas sprayed in their faces. I'd been telling my brief this all along and I think even she doubted my side of the story, and that the two police offers would not tell blatant lies to drop me in it.

Anyway, she pointed out to the judge that perhaps the two policemen involved were not, in fact telling the truth. After a break the judge came back and agreed with my barrister that the police were not telling the truth, so the case against me spraying them with gas was thrown out. But I was still found guilty of affray and of having a prohibited weapon. No matter how long or how hard you looked at the video evidence, there was no way, absolutely no way, that you could see clearly, me holding anything in my hands. The jury should not have found me guilty of the Prohibited Weapon charge because there was no evidence on the film, or anywhere else, that on that day I had carried and sprayed gas.

The judge sentenced me to nine months for the affray and nine months for the gas, both to run concurrently. I was also banned from football for another five years. I was gutted. I'd been fitted right up. It seemed they were out to get me. Debbie was in court and when I was sentenced, I looked over at her and she looked devastated. I'd done it again. I'd hurt the women I cared for, the mother of my kids. I was led away to the cells and Debbie was allowed to come down to speak to me before I was taken off to prison. She struggled to hold back the tears and I tried to reassure her that I'd only be away for a few months. I explained to her that if I behaved inside I'd be out after six months or even less, if I was lucky, and kept my head down.

I was the last one to be sentenced that day so I was taken by a car with a screw, to Dana prison in Shrewsbury; well actually, it was a taxi that took us. Because it was late they couldn't get hold of a prison service van so I arrived in style, well, a Vauxhall Cavaliar anyway!

Shrewsbury was just a holding prison, which was old and had just one main wing. It was a bit like Winston Green Prison in the terms that it was old and run down and full of convicts and I didn't get any grief in there. My case had been in the papers so a few people knew of me when I arrived. I even met a few Stoke lads in there who were as good as gold and helped me settle in.

After five weeks I was moved to Blakenhurst Prison, which was nearer to home, and in there it was home from home. I knew loads of people and the screws were O.K. If you didn't bother them, they tended to leave you alone. I had regular visits from Debbie, who seemed to be coping well under the circumstances. She was a strong girl but I really did miss her and the kids and hated being away from them all.

I was lying in my cell one night listening to the Ireland v England International being played at Lansdowne Road in Dublin. Now, anyone with an ounce of sense will tell you that whoever arranged this so-called "International Friendly" must have need his or her brains tested. It came as no surprise to even the most ordinary well-behaved football fan that doesn't get involved in any trouble in any shape, or form that it was going to go off big style at this fixture. The two teams hadn't played one another for a good few years over in Ireland. A lot of English fans have connections with Scotland's Glasgow Rangers, who are a mainly

Protestant-supported team, or I should say their support comes from mainly from the Protestant communities, both in Scotland and Northern Ireland. On the other hand their arch rivals, Celtic, draw most of their fans from the Catholic side of things in Scotland, Northern Ireland and Southern Ireland. So a lot of religious connotations were riding on this fixture, plus political parties from the rest of Britain like The British National Party and Combat 18 were, according to the tabloid press, also seen out there stirring up trouble. Whether they were or weren't it was going to go off no matter who or who wasn't there from certain right-wing parties. This fixture was a recipe for disaster. It gave the hardcore hooligan element the opportunity to show in some way, that by going to Dublin they weren't intimidated by the fact that the I.R.A. who supposedly have, a big Irish support could over the years bomb and kill innocent people on the mainland. They were there to support their national side and were there as Englishmen who were going to stand up and be counted.

At the game it was ironic but Ireland took the lead with a goal from our very own Wolves player, David Kelly, but that was the signal for the English fans in the seats in the upper stand to pelt the Irish fans down below them with anything they could lay their hands on. Bottles and glasses were thrown as seats were ripped up and used as missiles. It was a full scale riot, not helped by fighting between some fans pitch-side and the Irish Garda wading in with their truncheons and cracking anyone's skull within striking distance. No prisoners were taken as English blood was spilt that night. Revenge was short, sharp, and coloured red and sweet for some people. I pissed myself laughing as the game was, shock horror, abandoned. The radio commentator was near to tears as he described the scenes and spoke of how he was ashamed to be English. "Grow up ya cunt" I shouted at the radio. What did anyone honestly expect? The English and Irish fans to stand side by side with no hint of aggro? If anyone's to blame it's the pricks that arranged the fixture. Do they not watch the news on T.V. or read the papers? Who are the fucking morons in this instants?

Just along the landing from me in another cell, listening to the game was a fellow Wolves fan and top criminal, one-eyed dodgy Sean Milner. He was in for dodgy money he'd been caught in South Wales, and had been sentenced to 28 days inside and was sharing a cell with one of the many Smack-heads in there.

I'm released after doing six months of my nine-month sentence plus I end up doing another 3 months for further charges. I get back home and keep my head down and out of trouble, and try to bring a few bob into the house.

The year after my release, a mob of Wolves, including me, travel back up to Stoke for a game. We arrive in the city centre, and somehow evade the Old Bill, and take over two pubs. I'm banned, so after walking down to the ground and seeing no sign of a Stoke mob, me and me two mates, Dime Bar and Leyton, walked back to a nearby pub we'd just passed. As we walk through the main door, we see the place is packed with Stokes' main firm. We stop dead in our tracks we've frozen to the spot. They look at us with disbelief that we've walked into their boozer and we look at them with disbelief that we've found their boozer. We can't just turn around and walk out because we know that as soon as we do then they will burst out through the doors and come after us. There are three of us, and three hundred of them, and basically, we're fucked. We're in the lap of the Gods and I'm praying if there is a God let him get us out of here unscathed, please. One of their lads steps forward and pushes his face into mine we're nose to nose, head to head.

"Hello girls, how ya doing? He smiles and the blokes behind him laugh.

You're Gilly Shaw aint you? ".

"Am I?"

"Yes you are" he nods.

"Is that right?" I reply.

"You're in Stoke now".

"So what?"

Then in comes the Old Bill bursting through the doors. I think they were expecting to find a full-scale punch up in progress with us three getting the shit kicked out of us. They look disappointed and place us under arrest.

"What for?" I protest.

"Theft" replies one of the coppers.

"Theft of what?" I ask.

"Money from across the road".

They arrest us and take us to the police station where they strip search us and, as expected, find nothing. No evidence, nothing, fuck all. They keep us in the cells until 8.30 and then throw us out without charge.

We're walking up the road, back towards the train station, and we've all got the see through plastic bags with the gear inside that the Old Bill has taken away from us while we've been in custody. I'm taking me money out and putting it into the front pockets of my jeans, when around the corner come about 15 of Stoke's finest. Leyton backs off as I pull me leather belt out of the bag. "Come on Wolves," says one of them. Moving menacingly towards us, Leyton's back-pedalling and then comes back as he can see me and Dime Bar are going no-where as we prepare for them to come into us. I'm waving me leather belt around like a lunatic. A kick is aimed at Dime Bar, and as he moves backwards, to avoid it he trips over and they're on him in a flash. They land a few boots into his body as I smack one of them, and they back off. The Old Bill arrives and this Stoke lot are off like a shot.

"Why don't you just fuck off out of here?" shouts a copper, angrily.

"We're trying to" I reply.

He rounds us up with his arms open wide and hands out stretched like a farmer working a Border collie he only needed a sheep pen to guide us into.

Over the years I have got to know many of Stoke's main faces and they're top fellas. I have total respect for the likes of Jasper, Cossack, Jed, Robbie, Finbar, and the rest of Naughty 40, and a lot of their young lot who are as game as fuck but like many teams these days a lot of their main lads are on these banning orders. They always came to our place when they said they were coming, unlike some teams, and when I've been on England duty and met up with them they never come across as liberty takers with other English firms, you can rely on them 100%. Like I say, a top firm, a bit like my own side. We've both not had a lot to cheer about over the last few years, but what our two teams can't do on the field of play, trust me, both sets of fans can do it off of it.

CHAPTER SEVEN

EURO 96

The last three Wolves' games of the 95-96 season saw us draw at home 0-0 with Huddersfield Town in front of nearly 26,000, lose 3-0 away to Reading and the final game saw us draw 1-1 away to Charlton. Not a particularly good season as the Sleeping Giant stayed a kip and finished 20th. Piss poor in anyone's reckoning. Would we ever again see the days of the great players who wore the gold and black kit with so much pride, the likes of, Sir Billy Wright, Derek Dougan, Ray Crawford, Derek Parkin, John Richards, all great and fantastic players and terrific servants to the club.

The first major tournament in England for 30 years began with England playing their "Group-A" fixture at Wembley against unfancied Switzerland. Fans' expectations across the country were very high and dreams of another '66 Cup Triumph were how this tournament was being spoken about. I came down to London with a few mates by car. We knew there'd be no trouble so we came down just to take in the atmosphere. Central London was buzzing and we found a lively pub and watched the match on the big screen, but a 1-1 draw with the Swiss made us think "was it all worth it?"

Seven days later, we answered our own questions and were back down to London to see us play the Jocks. Now this was going to be a game and a half and any club with a hooligan following of any note would be out to make a show, 25 of our lot came down by train and the rest of us came down in two mini-buses. We parked up and headed for the Globe Pub on the corner of Baker Street, where traditionally, England fans have met up before big games at Wembley. As we breezed past, fans from various clubs were packed inside or standing outside on the pavement, with bottles of beer in their hands. Stone Island seemed to be the most popular badge of honour on show that day. Standing in amongst the crowds, like a cat staring into a car's headlights and frozen with fear as they spotted us on the prowl, was about 15 Albion lads. The look on their faces said it all it was a picture. They shit themselves but today was a day of unity. Personal squabbles were to be put to one side and club rivalries shelved. Today was the day we showed the Jocks who had the best firm. Gone were the days when they could come down to Wembley and take the piss. Thousands upon thousands of them used to descend on London dressed in kilts and tartan and you'd be hard pressed to find an Englishman inside the stadium. Look at the year they came on the pitch, ripped up the turf, took it away as souvenirs, and broke the crossbar down and pulled down the goal nets. Was that incident the reason why the Home Internationals ended?

We left the Albion boys to finish off the Dry Sherry or the glasses of Babycham or whatever it was they were drinking, and made our way to the Phoenix Pub, which is just off the Edgeware Road. When we arrived there was already about 50 boys and by 11.30 a.m. there was about 100, the bulk being made up of Chelsea, Stockport and Sheffield Wednesday. As the morning wore on, more and more people arrived until our numbers swelled to around 300. I looked around me and it was an awesome mob. Inside the pub was the cream of English hooligans if the devil could have cast his net, but by 1.30 the Old Bill or the Football Intelligence Unit cast theirs. They arrived in force, sealed off the front and back of the pub and after a stand off, proceeded to allow one person at a time to leave the pub. You were asked your name and address, searched, photographed, and if you could produce a match ticket, you were allowed on your way. If you had no match ticket, you were basically warned that if you came to the attention of the police any more that day then you would be nicked under a Section so and so. It was all bollocks. The rumours flying around before the Old Bill arrived were that the Jocks were drinking in pubs around the Camden area of North London.

Somehow, after leaving the pub I ended up with half a dozen Spurs fans and went with them to a nearby pub to watch the game on T.V. and what a game it was. After a very close, cagey 45 minutes, Steve McManaman began tormenting the Scottish defence with some magical wing play. The Jocks missed a penalty and Shearer and Gazza scored a goal apiece to seal a victory, and what a goal Paul Gascoigne's goal was. Arsenal's David Seaman had pushed Gary McAllister's penalty over the bar, and England quickly broke from the resulting corner. The ball was pushed out to Gazza who flicked it over Scottish defender, Colin Hendry's head, and before it could land, Gazza had followed the flight of the ball and smashed it passed the helpless Andy Goram. The pub erupted and England's official anthem of "Three Lions on the Shirt" echoed around the pub. Job well done! In addition, it was sung much better than Baddiel and Skinner could do it.

I followed the majority of the England fans from the pub and headed towards Trafalgar Square but before I could get into the already packed-solid square, I bump into Abbo and a few of the Wolves lads that had come down by train. They'd just had a bit of a stand off with a mob of Hibs and Partick Thistle Jocks. Thousands upon thousands of Englishmen were milling around and the Old Bill somehow pushed the Jocks into one corner of the square and then surrounded them. There was no way of getting near them. Bottles and glasses flew through the air as Japanese tourists clicked away happily with their flashing cameras. They didn't have a clue what was going on. They probably thought it was the English version of their T.V. game show "Endurance" and the idea of this particular game is to see how many direct hits with bottles Scottish people in their national dress could take! It's not long before the Old Bill have had enough and baton charge the advancing English fans back. A Scotsman in a tartan kilt and matching Tam-O-Shanter, with a big, bushy, ginger, beard, has strolled into the middle of our mob. He's completely unaware of what's going on but soon finds out as his skirt is lifted up and a swift kick up his bare arse sends him on his way. " Give us a kiss darling" shouts one wag. The Old Bill with force clear the square completely and various mobs of ours break off down side roads. The mob I'm with bumps into a 200 strong mob of English in Leicester Square. They'd just had a row with a 100 strong Jock mob outside the Hippodrome Night Club apparently they were as game as fuck and had flashed blades and cut one of our boys. Our lot had backed them off and then had them on their toes before the Old Bill broke it up with dogs. We wander around for a while and as we come out onto the Charing Cross Road, there's a stand off between two mobs. The traffic 'as come to a standstill and the mobs are facing one another through the gap in between two double Decker buses, a few of Chelsea's finest, along with a mixture of Q.P.R., are calling it on with 50 or so Middlesborough lads.

"Come on ya Northern cunts," shouts a cockney voice, bouncing up and down in the middle of the road. Again the Old Bill move in and break up this little spat. We've pushed up towards Tottenham Court Road and it looks as if the whole of London 'as come to a standstill as traffic is grid locked. A group of Forest lads come out of a side street and a few words and punches are exchanged, again the Chelsea faces are involved, it seems the Forest firm have taken exception to a Q.P.R. fan that's with the Chelsea lads.

"Get rid of that little cunt" growls a big burley thick set Forest lad. They have a history going way back with Rangers and old wounds and long memories are re-surfacing. With no Jocks to fight with, I knew it wouldn't be long before certain clubs turned on one another. A bloke with a mobile phone stuck to his ear, tells everyone within earshot that the Jocks are up at Kings Cross and are taking right liberties. It was like someone had just gave the order to start the London Marathon as thousands of bodies jogged off, a sea of heads could be seen bobbing up and down, heading northwards. The lazy bastards amongst us, including me, break off, having had enough exercise for the day, I dived down the tube. A couple of stops later and we were off the train and out onto the street, but by the looks of it the Old Bill have already tumbled our plans and are already there, keeping a close eye on things. Across the road a couple of Scotsmen dressed from head to toe in tartan, stand outside a pub drinking, and by the looks of it the Jocks' national restaurant, McDonalds, is heaving with them. A few English lads are strolling about, just waiting for something to happen, and then we hear a rumble and a roar in the distance as traffic stops and the mob we left back at Tottenham Court Road turns the corner and head our way. That's the signal for every down and out, tramp, dosser, Big Issue seller and

Scotsman caught out on the street to find a safe haven as they scamper away, in every direction. From a side road next to Kings Cross station, a crowd of Jocks appear throwing bottles at the English. A few brave ones amongst them run into the no-mans land gap and trade punches with obliging Englishmen. From the front of the station appears another mob of bottle-throwing Jocks, a few of them making a feeble effort to climb over the metal railings. It goes toe to toe before the Scots are backed off into the lobby of the station. These weren't the tartan wearing hordes; these were the casuals from Hibs, Aberdeen and Dundee, and were decked out in all the latest designer labels.

The night ends with more bottle throwing and more arrests. We've had a long day and the Old Bill were nicking anyone they didn't like the look of so we head back to meet the others where the mini-buses were parked.

The next game is against Holland, another country with a supposedly big hooligan element, but the word on the street is their boys won't be showing for this game so me and the rest of the Wolves lads watch it on the big screen in a pub in Wolverhampton. England have a tremendous result and beat the Dutch 4-1 with two goals apiece from Alan Shearer and Teddy Sherringham. The whole country comes alive that night with dancing in the streets, cars sounding their horns and birds flashing their tits. The morning after the game everyone seems to have a smile on his or her face. One football result and it showed it could pull the whole country together.

Next up was the quarterfinal game against Spain. We had topped "Group A" to go through and a place in the semis beckoned, but first a tough game against the Spanish. I travelled down to London with two carloads of lads and watched 90 minutes of drab, boring football on the T.V. in a West End pub. The game then went into extra time but this game was nothing like the free flowing football we'd played against the Dutch. This was a tense, complex performance and it looked like we were out when the Spaniards scored a goal, but to everyone's relief it was disallowed for offside. After 120 minutes, the game finishes 0-0. Now it was down to penalties. Stuart Pearce even strolled up to sink one. He showed some bottle and made up for his crucial penalty miss some six years earlier. Eventually we went through 4-2 on penalties and faced our old adversaries, West Germany, in the semis. This was one game I wasn't going to miss.

Sixty of us came down by train and we headed straight for the stadium. Around Wembley, you could sense the buzz and mobs from firms from all over the country were actively out and about. No one was that sure if the Germans would show. We got together with a mob from Huddersfield and an even bigger mob from Arsenal, who, I was told, was on the look out for a mob from their archrivals, Spurs. I didn't realise just how much those two teams hated one another. I'd put it on a par with us and West Brom or Villa and The Blues.

The game kicked off but there was still a massive mob walking around in the darkness outside the stadium. It was hard to make out who was who. Wembley isn't that well lit up especially along Wembley Way and the footpaths that lead from the vast car parks, so if we did happen to bump into a firm of Germans then we wouldn't know it until we were right on top of them. Most of the light outside comes from the hundreds of hot-dog and burger vans, which seemed to be spaced out every few yards, a bit like a wagon train you'd see in a cowboy film. The smell of onions filled the air as workers from the stalls took a fag break now that most people were inside the stadium. Ticket touts walked away, pockets bulging with money. £500 a ticket we'd heard a few of them quote but who can blame them if people are silly enough to pay it. After all, it's their job and they'd argue that they're supplying a service and that service for big, sold-out games doesn't come cheap. From inside the stadium after just minutes, we hear a roar, and a geezer with a transistor radio stuck to his ear tells us that Shearer 'as scored from a Gascoigne corner. "Fucking hell". We jump up and down and join in the celebrations.

"Come on England, Come on England" goes up the chant. Strangers cuddle one another and there's plenty of backslapping and hand shaking going on. For all I know the geezer I've just been hugging could be a West Brom fan. The thought sends shivers down my spine. The excitement soon calms down when word goes around that the Germans have equalised. The game goes into extra time with the score at 1-1. Tottenham's Darren Anderton hits the post with a shot and Gazza just fails to toe-poke the rebound into an empty net. The Germans have a Kuntz golden goal disallowed and it finishes all square, and once again, we're involved in a penalty shoot out. It's Gareth Southgate's turn to take one but his weak shot is straight at the German keeper who saves easily. Again we've been beaten by the Germans in a penalty shoot out as the German player Kuntz and the rest of the German cunts celebrate another victory over the old enemy as the Wembley crowd taunt the German fans inside the stadium by singing "Two World Wars and One World Cup". We head off to Trafalgar Square where trouble 'as already kicked off. A group of Carlisle lads, including Ken's nephew, are throwing bottles at the Old Bill. As more fans flood into the square, passing cars are kicked if they're a German design. A BMW and a Mercedes, parked at the roadside, have their windscreens smashed in, wipers bent and pulled off, and every light and panel dented and kicked. Anything German is seen as a target. People who are on their way home from the theatre or work are attacked in their German made cars. The police have seen enough and charge the rampaging mob. This is turning into a full-scale riot as a car is turned over and set on fire. I'm caught in no-man's land as it kicks off with the Old Bill I'm grabbed and wrestled to the floor as my new Burberry denim shirt is ripped off my back. I'm hit over the head with a police truncheon and fear the worst and as I'm pulled to my feet, I now expect to feel the cold steel of police handcuffs next on my wrists. As my head swims around and blood runs down my face I feel like I'm pissed, and I'm having trouble standing up on my own. Fuck me, that cunt did whack me with that truncheon. The cold night air is getting into the open gash and it's stinging like fuck. Next thing they've let go of me and they're off. Mobs of lads run pass me as they give chase to the fleeing coppers. I wipe my face and check my hand; my fingers are covered in blood.

"You alright mate?" asks a lad as he rushes past me a bottle in his hand, ready to launch.

"Yea mate, I'm fine" I replied. As I stagger off into the night.

Fuck me, did I have a sore head the next day!

CHAPTER EIGHT

NEW MAN = NEW DREAMS

After the disappointment of losing to the Germans at Euro '96, the national side had a change of management. Terry Venables had decided to stand down so that he could sort out his libel cases with Tottenham Supremo, Alan Sugar. In his place came Glen Hoddle, an ex Spurs player who'd left his job at Chelsea to take on the England coach's role. He had all the credentials and things looked promising but rumour had it that he wasn't the F.A.s first choice. Alex Ferguson was the man the hierarchy of English football wanted as Venables's successor, but the board at United told him that he would have to honour his contract.

Wolves kicked off the 96-97 season with a new man in charge, Mark McGhee. The former Leicester manager had come in at the back end of last season taking over from the departed Graham Taylor, and what a start he had. Steve Bull notched up a hat trick in the 3-0 win at Grimsby and followed that with the only goal in a 1-0 home win over Bradford City. As usual Bradford never turned up with any sort of firm, but then again, they've never turned up at our place. It was a fair old gate though with nearly 25,000 fans showing up.

In the September of that campaign we won handsomely, 4-2, at The Hawthorns. The Old Bill had it well sewn up and there was no real bother, we done the double over them that year when we beat them 2-0 at home in the January. We showed the shit in their Tesco carrier bag shirts just who the governors really are, and they have the neck to call us Dingles, the sad cunts. Birmingham at home saw the first bit of aggro for a long time when we lost the game 2-1 and 50 of their Zulus came the back way into Wolverhampton and attacked a pub with 80 of our lot inside. A No one saw them coming and all they did was throw a few bottles, which smashed outside, and then they did a runner before we could get out of the pub and a punch was thrown. They were rounded up straight away by the Old Bill and escorted away, but according to them sad cunts, they saw that as a result.

Over at their place in the March we took a right tidy firm and besides having it all, our own way out on the streets and in the city centre before and after the game, we also turned them over 2-1 on the pitch. Steve Bull and Don Goodman, both ex Baggies, scored for us. We also beat Stoke City at home 2-0 but lost away to them 1-0. The last game of that season saw us lose 1-0 at home to Portsmouth, who also knocked us out of the F.A. Cup 2-1, but we made it to the play-offs where we met Crystal Palace. In the first leg at Selhurst Park, it was a warm, May evening and we went down there with a 200 strong mob, on the pitch we got well-stuffed 3-1. The return leg 4 days later saw us win 2-1 but go out on goal difference. The big time had eluded us yet again. Our dreams were over for another year, our bubble burst, but I was sure we would be back again. Mark McGee had got the players believing in themselves and was turning out to be a good choice of manager; similar to Glen Hoddle and the job he was doing as the England Coach. He'd won his first three games in charge with wins in the World Cup qualifiers against Moldova, Poland and Georgia. His first loss came against the Italians at Wembley where we lost to a Gan-France Zola goal.

In the return game out in Rome, we needed a draw to ensure World Cup qualification. For this game, a few of us fly out from Gatwick. On the flight, there was about 25 Brentford boys who I never knew had any sort of firm I always thought they were like Wimbledon or Watford. We found digs to stay in and I dropped my bags off and went off out sight-seeing. The trouble with Rome is that once the tourists have all gone back to their hotels for their evening meal, then the whole place seems to shut down, and of a night there's fuck all happening. We did manage to find an Irish bar that stayed open late. They had a strange system in that you went to one part of the bar, ordered a drink and paid for it, you were then given a receipt and went to another part of the pub to get your drink. The thing was they only looked at your receipt before they handed it back to you, then they poured out your drink and handed it over. It didn't take the lads long to suss this so loads of us just paid for the one drink and kept going back up with the same receipt. We got pissed as parrots, absolutely fucking hammered. At the end of the night, as we staggered off back to the hotel, I heard a couple of Irish lads moaning about how expensive Rome was and how much they'd spent on booze in the Irish bar. I can't see why they call the Irish thick, can you? That night we'd met up with and drank with a good group of lads Stoke City and Huddersfield were just a couple of the firms out there in numbers but we had a good crack with both of them.

The day of the game we set off early to walk down to the stadium. In the street, up ahead of us, a group of English were rucking with a small mob of Italian youths. The Old Bill was there on the scene in seconds and broke it up. We came to a bridge where there were rows of hot dog stalls all chained together. Italian ticket touts were hanging around trying to sell their well over-priced match tickets. A group of Aston Villa lads stop us and we get talking. A few English lads start arguing with the locals about the price of the tickets, and one of the touts, as had enough and runs at me waving a bat around. That's it, it goes right off. One of the Italians is pushed into one of the hot dog stands, which turns on its side, but because they're all chained together, in turn the whole lot go over. The coppers rush in and throw a tear gas canister into the middle of us which breaks up the scuffle, as it clears I can see the stadium up ahead I wipe my face and rub my eyes and try to get focused. Laying on the floor next to me is an England fan.

"You all right mate?" I ask, as I help him to his feet.

"Yea I'm all right" he replies, and his accent is the same as mine.

"Where ya from?" I ask him

"West Brom" he replies. Fuck me I should have let the cunt go, a fucking Baggie and I'm helping him to his fucking feet. I say no more and walk away, shaking my head. When we reached the stadium those of us that didn't have tickets tried rushing the gates. The Old Bill baton charge us back, it was going off mental and a few English lads were being dragged away by the police.

"Fucking help them", someone shouted, and we ran at the Old Bill who let go of their captives.

"Do the Old Bill" was another shout, but a few of them must have understood English and out came the batons and the gas. Perhaps not, and we wander off, a mate of mine had got hold of a match ticket for me so in we both went, and we soon noticed that there were Englishmen in every part of the ground. Some newspapers had reported that there'd be 16,000 English fans attending the game. I don't know about that but there were thousands of English lads out there. This was the days before face painted fans with Union Jack flags draped over their shoulders. This was when England had a top mob. When it kicked –off inside the stadium the Italian fans were standing on their seats to crane their necks to watch the English fans battling with their police.

"Sit down yaw cunts" I was shouting. I was going fucking mad as a pocket of Englishmen did battle in the far corner. The noise inside was unbelievable, the atmosphere electric. I'd put it on a par with the Bescot stadium at Walsall (only joking!). No, it was some stadium, probably the best I've been to. When the teams came out to start the game I swear if there'd been a roof on it, it would have been lifted off by the volume of noise. "Ingerland", "Ingerland", "Ingerland", "Ingerland" was matched by chants "Italia", "Italia", "Italia", "Italia". It was just amazing. This made the trip so worthwhile. I soaked up the atmosphere and it made you proud to be English and like most Englishmen that had made the trip over here, I saw myself as a sort of ambassador representing my country.

Paul Ince was captain for the night and in the opening minutes you could see Hoddle had set his stall out and was packing the middle of the park with players who would fight and scrap for everything. David Batty put in some crunching tackles early on and Paul Ince and Gazza lifted the players around them. The first half ends 0-0 and then out came the teams for the second period. If only we could hold on. I'd be happy with 0-0 but it would still be nice to cheer an England goal, just to shut these cunts up sitting around me. No matter how hard the Italians pressed, they could find no way through the English defence, which was superbly marshalled by the excellent Tony Adams. Paul Ince had to go off to have a cut on his head bandaged up, his white England shirt covered in blood. As he re-appeared his never-say-die attitude was recognised by the England faithful who welcomed him back with a roar of approval. Near the end, the Italian centre forward, Casiraghi, sent a header agonisingly close. He never did have a lot of luck. He later moved to Chelsea for five million pound where he scored one goal, broke his leg and had to retire from football through injury. When the final whistle went, the celebrations were wild. We'd qualified for the World Cup finals, which were to be held in France.

We came out of the stadium and there were rows upon rows of Old Bill, many dressed in full riot gear. They'd placed metal barriers along the route they wanted us to take. Me and a few of the others picked one up and ran at the coppers with it. They parted like a hot knife through butter and we were away. Police sirens filled the air as local youths hung around on street corners, but as soon as we approached, they were off. Before the game, rumours were abounding that a few English had been slashed. Ask any Liverpool fan what they think of the youth of Rome. The Scousers had played Roma, one of the local sides, in a European Cup final at the Stadio Olympico. Before and after the game there were reports that quite a few Liverpool fans had been attacked with knives and by the sounds of it nothing had changed. It wasn't long before the Old Bill surrounded us and put us onto coaches. To tell ya the truth it was getting boring keep chasing gangs of Italians about, and I was getting pissed off every bar and restaurant we passed was either closed or for Italians only. As soon as the coach I was shoved on pulled away, the bottles, bricks and rocks smashed into it from outside. The Italian Old Bill stood by and let their fellow countrymen do whatever they wanted, some even stood by laughing, as we ducked down inside the coaches. We'd had enough, and rushed to the front of the coach and pulled the front door open.

"No, No, No", shouted the driver, and as he slowed down with just one eye on the road and one on me as I took aim with the glass I had in my hand, I steadied myself to launch it at a group of bottle throwing Italians we were just about to pass. Unfortunately, I slipped in the gangway and the glass smashed into the windscreen of the coach. The driver went fucking mad. I don't know what he was saying but he was shouting his head off, screaming and was near to tears. You know how

emotional these Latin types can get, right fucking drama queens! The
Old Bill jumped on board and we all scampered back to our seats. They
pick out a kid from Middlesborough who they arrest and lead away. If
you ever read this I'm sorry mate.

We're dumped off the coach near the central train station, which is well
handy for us, as we have to catch a train to Pisa, which is about five
hours away. From there, we plan to get our flight back to Gatwick. We
arrived in Pisa around mid afternoon after being fucked around by the
Old Bill in Rome and check into a hotel, which is top class. After a quick
kip and a shower, we go out sight seeing and take some pictures of the
leaning tower what a waste of time that is. After a few beers in various
bars, twelve of us end up in a Chinese restaurant I went off for a quick
piss and on me way out of the toilets, I noticed a load of bottles of vodka
stacked up in the corner, when I got back to my seat I tell the rest of the
boys on what I've seen and a few of them order bottles of water from the
waiter, they drink the water, and go off to the toilet and fill the empty
bottles up with Vodka. We then start ordering fresh orange juice to go
with the Vodka and get as pissed as parrots. The Chinks are pissing
themselves laughing about the mad English getting well pissed on
mineral water. We slowly finished the meal and one by one drifted off
into the night with out paying. In part of the hotel, they are having
building work carried out so, me being a nosey bastard, I have a look
through the tins of paint and the wallpaper. In amongst it all was a
security camera and a bag of Polyfilla. Just for a joke I put the filler
inside the camera and hide it in the bottom of Steve Preston's bag who
we call "The Rat" He goes through Customs at Pisa no problem, but
when he arrives back at Gatwick he's pulled to one side by Customs
officers who turn his case upside down and find the hidden camera
with the goods hidden in it, which looks suspiciously like cocaine. He
looks at me, red-faced, as a Customs officer dangles it in front of his face
and asks him if he can explain what's inside the bag.

"You bastard", The Rat mouths in my direction. We're all in hysterics.
Even the Custom man tries hard not to laugh and he is let off.

I get back home to Debbie, and the kids, drop my bag off, and head
round to Nan's. She hasn't been well lately and she's been diagnosed at

the hospital with having breast cancer. She's now living all alone in her big house but all my aunts and uncles, cousins and her friends, pop in and out visiting her. I just pray she will be all right.

The 97-98 season kicked off with us losing 3-2 at home to Oldham with Steve Bull notching a brace. We played the likes of West Ham, Portsmouth, Hull City, Newcastle, and Leicester, but during that whole season, apart from the odd scuffle, there was no real trouble both home and away. The biggest row we had that season was in the F.A.Cup, up at Elland Road against Leeds United. It was in March and I was on holiday out in Tenerife with the family but I phoned Dave Colley who's one of the lads and was at the game and as I was talking to him, I could hear it going off in the back- ground. When I got back home the lads that were there told me it had gone mental up at Leeds and that we had turned them over big time, but that wouldn't be the first time we've turned them over up at their place. About 82 Fingles, and one of his coaches went into Leeds main boozer "The Peacock" and smashed them to pieces. At this cup game we took about 60 up there on the train as we came out of the station they were waiting for us and there was a few scuffles the Old Bill broke it up and put our lot on buses to the ground. That day we had Hans Segers the ex Wimbledon goalkeeper playing for us and he even saved a Jimmy Floyd Hasselbaink penalty, Segers was reported to have been involved in Match fixing a few years back but he played a blinder in this game as we won 1-0 with a goal from Yorkshire man and life long Leeds fan Don Goodman. Afterwards, a few of us came out on to the street, and a 100 strong mob of Leeds were waiting across the road, the Old Bill were watching what was going on, so we told the Leeds lot to walk further up the road away from the Gavvers, as we got to the Billy Bremner statue they came at us from all sides. There were only 60 of us and about 200 of them, but only about 20 of their lot stood and had a go. As we got further up the road, some of them come back tooled up with fucking red and white plastic traffic cones they threw them at our lot then they legged it again. Carl me mate, was one of the back markers, and as he set off on the long walk back to the main line station he could hear foot steps behind him, without looking around he said "come on, hurry up" and as he looked around because there was no answer a Leeds fan who'd crept up on him smacked him in the mouth and ran off. It seemed the serious faces from all clubs just wanted to keep their heads down, avoid arrest, and make it out to the World Cup '98 in France.

CHAPTER NINE

FRANCE '98

England winning a World Cup in football is something most fans have never seen unless you were around in 1966. We've all seen the Geoff Hurst, was it or wasn't it over the line goal, and remember that famous quote of "they think it's all over" as Sir Geoff hammered home the fourth goal. This country winning another World Cup would be fantastic, a dream come true. The 1998 World Cup finals were to be held in France and England were kicking off their campaign in Marseille, against Tunisia. Even before a ball had been kicked, there was controversy when Paul Gascoigne was left out of the squad. Hoddle was reported to have said that Gazza was looking tired, mentally and physically. England won the opening game against Tunisia 2-0 with goals from Alan Shearer and Man. United's ginger nut, Paul Scholes. Nearly fifty five thousand were packed into the stadium with thousands more English outside watching it in bars and on a giant screen laid on by the French authorities. Trouble had flared the day before the game with fights between England fans and Arab and black local immigrants. As usual, the police stood by, watched, and done nothing that is until their boys were getting a bit of a pasting and then it was time to go into the England fans with gas and batons.

The day of the game saw crowds of topless England fans, many in shorts, soaking up the sunshine and the atmosphere without a hint of trouble. Masses of French riot Old Bill stood a couple of hundred yards away. They looked bored and pissed off, because they had no misbehaving Englishmen to deal with. That was until a hundred strong group of Arabs banging drums and waving Tunisian flags were allowed to walk past and goad the English masses. I ask ya, why didn't the French Old Bill intervene and stop them or even re-route them away from the English? No. I tell you why, because the Old Bill and certain English newspapers wanted to see the English fans caught up in more bother. As the Tunisians slowed down the first bottles were thrown. A few Arabs were punched and kicked and French knives were flashed. It escalated with gas being used to disperse the crowds and French snatch squads diving in and arresting so-called English ringleaders.

I'd been on the English scene now for a good few years and these people who were arrested, and had their faces splashed across the front pages of the English tabloids, were hardly what I'd call ringleaders. To be honest they were nobodies just normal geezers that had been caught up in a row. They were in the wrong place at the wrong time it was as simple as that. Having a shaved head a few tattoos and a beer belly doesn't necessarily qualify you to be one of the leaders of England's mob abroad, regardless of what the S-n or the Daily ———— might write.

Two mini-buses left Wolverhampton and drove down to the ferry port at Dover. There to meet and greet us were a mixture of Customs and British and French Old Bill. They asked to see our passports and asked all sorts of questions as to where we were off to. "Holland" came the reply from our bus, "Holland for a stag do". The French coppers viewed our replies with suspicion, our passports were taken from us and the coppers disappeared into an office while we sat in the motors. Ten minutes later they were back to inform us that sixteen out of the seventeen on our mini-bus had football-related convictions.

"Mr. Shaw and Mr. Abbots could you please make yourselves known to us". Me and Abbo looked at one another and stuck our hands in the air. "Follow me gentlemen" said one of the French Old Bill, sounding very much like Peter Sellers from the Pink Panther films. He strode off and we followed him into the office. Sitting behind a desk was an English copper. He looked at me and then looked at my passport, which he studied for what seemed like ages. He stamped it and handed it back to me. "Enjoy your stag party, Mr Shaw". I smiled.

"Mr Abbot, you're not going nowhere, there's an outstanding warrant for your arrest for an incident up at Port Vale". Abbo was then arrested and that was his World Cup over before it had even started. The first van was allowed through and we, unbelievably, although not allowed to travel to France, were allowed to catch the Sea Cat to Ostend in Belgium. We phoned the others and told them to meet us in Belgium. Another group of our lot were on a train, so they were also told about the change of plans and they to re-routed to Belgium.

We arrived in Ostend and went straight through Belgium Customs unchallenged. Overall and by various modes of transport, there was a mob of about 70 out there and our numbers from the Midlands was swelled even more by about 30 of Leicester City's finest. Big Rich and Tony Harrison were amongst a good set of their lads who joined up with us. We all were settled in a bar after finding digs. I was sharing a room with an Arsenal lad, Paul Bracken, who lived in Wolverhampton and was a Gooner, but I never did hold that against him. He was a top lad and a good mate of mine. On the T.V. was Belgium playing someone or other and one minute we've got half an eye on the game and the other eye on the fanny in the bar next minute everyone's going fucking mental, as fighting breaks out with some of the locals. Chairs are being thrown at the optics behind the bar and a barstool is hurled through the front windows. It's fucking bedlam as someone shouts that the Old Bill is on their way. Now the Belgium Old Bill are one mob you don't want to be fucking with because they are ruthless bastards who take no prisoners. A Belgium geezer once told me that to get into the Belgium Old Bill you had to be a crook. Say no more.

"I think it's time to go," I said to Paul as we headed out the door and up the road. Police vans and cars with sirens blaring and blue lights flashing, screech to a halt outside the building that was once used as a bar. The fighting had now spilled outside onto the pavement as the Old Bill steamed in, truncheons drawn, as English heads waited to be cracked.

Next morning we are up early and out, and after breakfast in some little shit hole we got talking to some Chelsea and Blackburn Rovers' lads.

We find out that after last night's bother 25 of our lot have been deported. We gather everyone from our mini-buses together that's not been nicked and drive across the border into France and down towards Lens where England are playing their third game of Group G against Colombia. Four days previously in Toulouse we'd lost our second game against Romania 2-1. Michael Owen had come on as substitute for Teddy Sherringham and equalised after England had gone a goal behind after just a few minutes into the second half. The game looked like it would end in a draw but Chelsea team-mates England's Graeme le Saux and Romania's Dan Petrescu, went for the same ball and Petrescu somehow managed to squeeze the ball through David Seaman's legs and into the back of the net for the Romanian winner. The England players couldn't believe it and now everything rested on the last game against Colombia.

As we drove through the streets of Lens trying to find somewhere to park, we noticed a group of what looked like English lads being chased along the road by a load of French Arabs. "Pull over" someone shouted and our two vans pulled over and stopped. We piled out and went straight into these French geezers. The lads that were being chased stopped running and gave us a hand as we ran the Frogs up the road. We gave up the chase after a couple of hundred yards and stopped for a breather, a round of applause broke out from the lads we'd just saved.

"Cheers lads" shouted a few of them. Putting their thumbs in the air

"Where ya from?" I asked.

"Birmingham" came back the reply. They were fucking Blues fans and we'd just saved their bacon.

"Where yowl from?" asked one of them, his nasal tones giving away where he was from.

"Wolverhampton" I replied.

Anyway, for just a few moments we let bygones be bygones and started chatting to them. It turned out they'd just had a row with a firm from Derby County followed by this little spat we'd just witnessed. The French Old Bill arrived and let off some gas and moved everyone on.

In the City it was a non-alcohol day with the bars that were open only selling soft drinks or tea and coffee. We settled down in a back street bar and watched the game on T.V. Hoddle had made some changes for this game by leaving out David Batty and bringing in Man. Utd's golden balls, David Beckham. He also swapped Owen in place of Sherringham and it worked. We were 2-0 at half time with goals from "Sick note" Darren Anderton and a Beckham "special" from a free kick. England sailed through the rest of the game, comfortable winners.

After finishing second in the group we were through to the knockout stages where we were paired with our old enemies, both on and off the field of play, Argentina. The two teams would meet in St-Etienne and everyone to a man knew what this game meant to both sides. We'd had the Argies kicking our boys to fuck in the 66 World Cup and even Sir Alf Ramsey branded them as animals. We'd had the Falklands War and the infamous Maradona and his hand of God so there was enough bad feeling between the two countries. I doubt very much if Glen Hoddle would have to give much of a team talk to raise his troops, maybe a "get out there and kick their arses" Would be sufficient.

Anyway, nearly 31,000 were packed into the compact stadium, with millions around the world glued to their T.V. sets. The game kicked off and you could almost touch the atmosphere coming out of the T.V. screen. It was electric and it seemed as if the whole country had come to a standstill to take time out to watch this game. The bars and pubs were packed to the rafters, shops closed, restaurants empty and the streets deserted. Within a couple of minutes of the start though, it all went terribly wrong when the Argies were awarded a very fucking dubious penalty. David Seaman was adjudged to have bought down Simeone, but it looked as though he tripped over Seaman and gone down far too easily. Batistuta, the Argentinean centre forward with the long, greasy hair who was now plying his trade in Italy, stepped up and tucked the spot kick away. Those fucking smug Argie bastards fucking loved it. As they kissed and cuddled one another I shouted at the screen, "fuck you, you greasy, no-good cunts", but they took no notice and carried on celebrating the goal. I don't think they could hear me. It wasn't long before Lady Luck shone on us, and Michael Owen burst into their box and was brought down by a last ditch challenge. "Penalty" shouted the entire pub, and the referee agreed as he pointed to the spot. Up stepped Alan

Shearer who paused a moment before slamming the ball into the net. 1-1 and it's game on.

"Ingerland", "Ingerland", "Ingerland" echoed around the pub. It's a close game until Owen picks the ball up just over the halfway line. He glides past two Argentian defenders before unleashing a fierce shot across goal and into the net. Fucking hell, the pub erupts. Beer and drink go everywhere, everyone's jumping up and down, strangers hug and kiss. I look around for a decent bird to have a cuddle and a snog with. There's no way I'm kissing some hairy-arsed geezer.

"Ingerland", "Ingerland" the whole place is proud of our boys as we sing our hearts out. Paul Scholes misses a golden chance to make it 3-1 and then just before half time the Argies are awarded a free kick on the edge of our area. David Seaman instructs the men in front on him on how many he wants in the defensive wall. Up steps, Zanetti who whacks the ball through a gap in the wall created by teammate, Ortega, and past the incensed David Seaman who can't believe his teammates' lack of concentration. The ref blows for half time. It's been some 45 minutes of football. Shortly after the re-start David Beckham is fouled and falls to the ground. As he lies there, he kicks out his foot and catches Simeone on the leg. Beckham jumps to his feet only to see the referee holding up the red card. He's been sent off for violent conduct and with that all our dreams and aspirations went with him but give the team credit, even with 10 men we held on through the 90 minutes and into the end of extra time. Then it was down to the dreaded penalty shoot-out, something over the years we've been absolutely shit at, and nothing had changed. Paul Ince missed one, as did David Batty, and we were out 4-3 on penalties.

A damp squid hung in the air as we trudged dejectedly out into the warm, June night air. Still, there was always Wimbledon tennis to watch on the telly. That would make up for a disappointing World Cup. I don't think, but it seems to me we have a team that seems to have no pride in wearing the England shirt and constantly bottling it on the big occasion. That night finished with the usual bottle throwing clashes with the Old Bill, as clashes with the police were reported almost up and down the country. With no Argentinean cars around to kick the wing mirrors off or smash the windscreens and with no Argentinean restaurants or bars to attack, the next best thing or the only thing to do was to boycott Argentinean tins of corn beef.

Within six months Hoddle was gone. His book "The World Cup Diary" caused quite a stink but his fate was sealed in an interview he gave to The Times in which in it he claimed that people born disabled were paying for sins in a previous life. I found that most distasteful and personally took exception to those comments. Within 48 hours of the article appearing, Hoddle jacked it in. He then issued a statement acknowledging that he made "a serious error of judgement". Since leaving the England set-up, it appears that wherever Hoddle has gone the team he has taken over has struggled. He did relatively little at Southampton, then went back to Spurs as the Prodigal Son who would return the glory days to White Hart Lane, and again did nothing, and was seen as a failure by many. It would seem he has some kind of curse on him. Maybe some kind of gypsy curse, but don't look at me. I'm not responsible if he has had a Romany curse put on him. Don't forget that as we write this he's now the manager of my team, Wolves, so maybe it's been temporarily lifted. We hope so anyway!

Wolves kicked off the 98-99 season with a 2-0 home win against Tranmere Rovers. We then went on a bit of a run by winning 2-0 away to Oxford Utd, followed by a 1-0 home win against Swindon Town, next up was a 2-0 away win at Watford, with Steve Bull grabbing his second goal of the campaign. We then drew 2-2 with Stockport County at home, and then, the run ended away to Port Vale where we lost 2-1.
In the September England lost in a European Championship qualifier in Stockholm against Sweden 2-1, with Alan Shearer getting the goal for England. In the October, we then draw 0-0 with Bulgaria at Wembley, in another qualifying game.

In my own life things just couldn't get any worse my Nan at 86 years old sadly passed away she was in the New Cross hospital with an infection caused by blood poisoning and we were all around her bed as she slipped away. I was devastated she was big, big influence on my life and

I loved that lady to bits she was everything to me rolled into one, she was my Nan first but she was like a Mum and a best friend. We had a big Gypsy funeral for her and over 200 people came to pay their respects she's forever in my heart and there's not a day goes by when I don't think about her or laugh out loud when I think of a stroke she'd pulled.

I was earning a decent living selling all the snide gear. Stone Island, Burberry, Boss, Armani are all good sellers, as are all the lines in fake designer gear. I sold enough men's gear, ladies bags, tops and sunglasses, to pay for my next trip abroad to see England play Luxembourg in another Euro qualifier.

Me, Gary Painton and Pecker set off for Luxembourg in Preston's silver Ford Granada. Fuck me we do look good. We're like something out of the 70s T.V. cop show "The Sweeney". We look just like Reagan and Carter sitting in the front, and as we drive along, I drop the window and shout at passers-by in my best Reegan growl, "shut up, you're nicked". We head for Dover and catch the boat across to Calais we roll off the other end but it aint long before we're lost. We study the map but we're none the wiser. We have it upside down, back to front, and inside out. We're well and truly lost; we screw the fucking thing up and I nearly chuck it out of the window but we carry on driving and after a couple of hours we find ourselves in Paris. We drive around the ring roads and past every famous landmark and I'm beginning to feel like Alan Whicker, on tour. More by luck than judgement we find ourselves on the road for Luxembourg, and when we arrive at the border the Old Bill are up ahead checking all the cars. One of our lot has a bag of Charlie on him and he won't get rid of it out of the window. If we're caught with it we're going to be in some serious shit and end up doing time so we pull out of the queue of cars crossing into Luxembourg, and he starts putting the gear up his nose. He wants to get rid of the evidence. Now we're being waved back into the queue by the border guards but Mr. Chang is still powdering his nose so we reverse back and he tries to get back into the queuing cars further back along the line. A copper waves us forward and we hold our breath thinking the games up, we've been spotted. However, he then waves us straight through, past everyone else and its foot down as we zoom off into the dark, damp, Luxembourg night. The copper must have thought that we'd already been checked and the car searched. A result!

We arrived in Luxembourg City, and after tramping around for what seemed like hours, we still couldn't find any B&Bs or hotels that were willing to take us, as soon as they heard our English accents they would claim that they were already fully booked. So we then hit on the idea of driving across the border into nearby Germany, which was only 20 miles away. We headed for the small border town of Trier, which is set on the banks of a river. We found a top hotel and booked in for two nights. This place is very plush and is the dogs bollocks. To good for us riff-raff but then again our moneys as good as anyone else's.

The next day, after a good night's kip and some top grub in the hotel, we set off for the game. England had only been allocated about 1200 tickets but there are about three thousand fans out here. The tiny stadium only holds about 8,000 so the bars in the city centre were packed with fans watching the game on telly. We get chatting and drinking with 15 to 20 Wigan lads things start to get a bit boisterous and it's not long before a fight starts with the locals who, by the looks of it, are mostly African immigrants. However, it soon fizzles out when the Old Bill turn up and the bar owner threatens to close. When the game starts, everyone settles down to watch the match and for once, I'm glad I'm not out there in the stadium as it is pissing down with heavy rain and freezing cold. It's still only October, but fuck me it's cold. Goals from Southgate, Shearer and Owen give us a victory in an otherwise dour game. At the final whistle, we drink up and jump back into the motor and head for the German border, I can't wait to get back to a bit of luxury.

The next morning two of us are up early and before we have breakfast we've packed and have the car loaded and ready to go. The other two stroll down as we're leaving the restaurant, and we go to reception and ask for the bill. They add it all up and present it to us. We glance at it, see the price, look at one another, and tell the girl on reception that we've accidentally packed our credit cards in with our luggage, which is now in the car. We stroll out towards the car with a "be back in a minute", we open the car door, stick the key in the ignition, start her up and we're off. We wheel spin out of there at high speed a trail of dust in our wake. We've pissing ourselves laughing at the stroke we've just pulled.

"Did you see the price of that bill?" As we pass the front doors of the hotel the other two are running down the drive behind us we slam the car into reverse and seconds later the other two jump in the back with their gear and we're off, Sweeney-style, only this time we're the villains who've just done a blag. Somehow, Chitty Chitty Bang Bang gets us back to Wolverhampton.

A couple of days later I get a phone call from Pecker.

"Here Gil, you know that hotel in Germany, we stayed at? Well they've only taken the money we knocked them for off my credit card. I just got a statement from my bank. They must have taken the details and the card number when I bought a drink from the bar the first night we were there".

"You fucking dick" I replied, trying not to laugh. "You should be more careful with ya card".

The phone went dead.

That 98-99 season ended with us finishing a very disappointing 7th in Division 1. We finished 8 points behind rivals Birmingham City who finished 4th. We went out of the F.A. Cup in round four to Arsenal. Sunderland finish as champions in Division One. Robbie Keane finished as our top scorer and Colin Lee took over from the departed Mark McGhee. After a promising start to the season we only win once in our last 7 games. The last 4 games see us draw 1-1 with the shit from up the road, draw 1-1 away to Bolton, draw 0-0 away to Grimsby, and lose 3-2 in the final game at home to Bradford. What can I say?

CHAPTER TEN

SUNNY BEACH

One of the European Championship qualifying games was out in Sofia in June, so 60 of us Wolves lads booked a weeklong holiday break in the Bulgarian, Black Sea resort of Sunny Beach. Twenty of us flew out from Liverpool airport and the rest followed the day after. The first lot out there had had a little tussle with a dozen or so Albion lads and they'd nicked their England flag with West Brom on it, and set it on fire. Needless to say, after that they kept right out of our way and kept a low profile. They know who's the boss.

When we arrived we soon realised that the resort was more Ryhl than Benidorm and our hotel, The Continental, was more the Bronx than Broadway. It was a right shit hole, but the beer, at 17p a pint, eased the pain of staying there. We'd only been there half an hour when one of our lot got into a row with one of the locals who pulled out a gun and pointed it at his head, and threatened to shoot him, welcome to Bulgaria!

We were changed into our tee shirts, shorts and flip-flops, and go out for a walk around and see what's what. We've heard on the hoolie grapevine that quite a few English fans are planning to stay in Sunny Beach resort and travel up to the Bulgarian capital, Sofia to watch the game, something we were also planning on doing. When we were having a stroll around the resort a few of our younger lot were a good couple of hundred yards in front of us. Sitting outside a bar were a dozen or so Bristol City lads. One of them overhears our accents.

"Fuck off you Brummie cunts" he shouts at the top of his voice and with that they throw glasses and bottles at us. Plastic tables and chairs go flying as holidaymakers scream and get out of the way a bit lively. We steam straight into them and I don't think they realised just who we were and how many of us there was. A couple of them get put on their arses and do the wise thing and stay down as we chase the rest of them up the road. The bar owner was going mad as his best glasses and plates and dishes and furniture is wrecked. The older ones amongst us give up the chase after 20 yards. Running at speed aint my game and I was soon fucked and gasping for breath. The younger ones were more energetic and carried on the chase, but after a couple of hundred yards they too give up and begin to turn around and walk back up the road to rejoin up with us. As they walk pass another bar, the doors burst open, and a mob appear chucking glasses and bottles at them.

"Su, Su, Suicide Squad", they chant as 25 of Burnley's top boys fancy a fight. Our young lot are as game as fuck and before we can get there, they have steamed into them and forced Burnley back up to the doors of the pub. Now we're all over them like fucking ants and they have no chance and nowhere to run I crack one geezer and send him sprawling. Fans from other clubs, who had been drinking inside, jump the bar to get away from the trouble. A heavy wooden table is picked up and thrown through the front window. We smash Burnley to pieces. Police sirens fill the air and soon the flashing blue lights arrive outside the bar. Fighting is still going on as copper pulls his gun from his leather holster, points it into the air, and two loud cracks ring out. He's let off two warning shots as everyone scarpers in every direction.

On the day of the game, we set off early morning for the 8-hour drive to the capital Sofia, in a fleet of hired mini-buses, and what a fucking boring drive, there's only so many mountains, valleys, forests and rivers, you can look at and stay remotely interested. We pasted a sign that read "Belgrade" so we weren't that far away from war torn Yugoslavia when we reached the stadium what a disappointment that was. It was a right shit- hole, which was nothing more than a big concrete bowl we were just going in with another mob of England fans. When Ned Kelly, an English copper who was on duty out there as a football intelligence spotter, stopped us.

"Hello Mr. Shaw and Mr. Abbots, we wondered where you'd been".

The Bulgarians, we heard, had two mobs. One was the Red Communist lot that followed C.S.K. Sofia, and the other, was Lefski. They all had their hoods on their coats pulled up and scarves wrapped around their faces, so that they couldn't be identified, but they did fuck all really and never posed a serious threat to us lot. They were total crackpots, who basically, just stood and stared at us all through the game. The match finished 1-1 with good old faithful, Alan Shearer, once again getting on the score sheet. There were only 22,000 fans in the stadium and to be truthful, it was a complete waste of time.

Afterwards we had the long journey back to Sunny Beach and what a fucking boring drive that was even worse then going there. We drove through the night in the darkness, and it was pitch black and I swear we never saw another soul on the road all the way back after we left Sofia. It's a journey I wouldn't be in a hurry to repeat. I've done some stupid things in my time and this was one of them. When we arrived back at the hotel I was, cream crackered and the next morning was in no rush to get up out of my bed. Around midday, I woke up and could see the sun shining in through a crack in the curtains so I decide to I get up and go down to the bar and have a quick bite to eat, and I have a glass of fresh orange juice and I'm then ready to face the world. I'm not the type to get up in the morning and drink pots of tea or coffee. I'm the compete opposite; I can't stand the stuff. Half a dozen of us are fed up sitting around the cruddy pool so decide to have a stroll around town and do a bit of shopping. I'm looking in a shop window for something for Debbie and the kids when a scuffle breaks out behind me. I turn around to see what's going on and one of our lads, Belly the Fireman, is rubbing his face, like he's just been hit, standing in front of him is a group of about 30 lads. Straight away I recognise them as the Burnley boys that we had the little spat with the other day. A big, fat lump amongst them stands at the front, his hands held up in a boxing pose.

"Come on Wolves, yaw bully cunts, let's have it now, you're nothing you cunts. Another one of theirs steps forward and I notice straight away he's got a bit of a gammy leg as he limps towards us. I don't catch

Me and Nicky
bigdick in Athens

Me and the lads in
Athens just before
it kicked off

The Wolves Youth out on St George's Day

The old bill stand and watch as a West Brom pub is attacked

Me and the lads out in Amsterdam, 2002

Our firm in Sheffield, 2002

Nosha, away – Sheffield United, 2002

Our mate Clive, good luck in the future

Fingles being laid to rest, God bless you mate

Me, Dava, Rob, Colley and Norman down in Cardiff

Me and the
Plymouth lads in
Cardiff for the
play-off final

Nicky Smith and
the two Abbos
on our way to
Boro

Half our firm at North Halaton on the way to the Boro

Jason Marriner, Martin King and me up in Nottingham

My son Adam and me, 2005

Job done, me and Kingy

what his surname is when he announces that his name is Johnny so-and-so, and it's his birthday. Fuck me, if I'd have remembered I would have sent him a card and I'm sure the boys if they had of known would have had a whip round and got him a present. Who gives a fuck if it's his birthday? And the way them cunts speak. They say we speak funny but they beat us, another one of theirs kicks one of ours up the arse and it looks for a moment that its going to kick-off and I'm not making excuses here, but we were hardly dressed for a row. A couple of us had nothing on their feet and I only had on a pair of flip-flops, not the ideal gear to start fighting in. We back off with the Burnley lads shouting insults and telling us what we'll get if they see us again. I'm fucking fuming. I head straight back to the hotel, storm up to my room, and put on a pair of trainers and round up the others. Those sitting around the pool are up and ready in seconds, those eating in the restaurant push their half finished meals to one side and join us. One of the lads goes and rounds up the boys sunbathing down on the beach and a few boys have their bedroom doors rapped on, and they have to leave their new-found Bulgarian fiancés in a state of undress.

"Right, let's go and show them liberty taking cunts" I say, as we march out of the hotel and back to where, less than 20 minutes ago, Burnley had given it the biggen.

We find the bar where they'd come from but besides an old couple sitting outside having tea and cakes, the place is now deserted. The waiter comes out points up the road and in broken English tells us that our friends have gone. We scour the resort looking for them. We check every bar, pub, restaurant and café and some places we even check twice. We searched the beach but it seems these cunts have vanished; into thin air, they've fucked off a bit lively. One of our lot comes up with an obvious quote of "they know what they're going to get when we find them". We've been searching for hours with no luck so we decide to go and have a beer back at The Red Lion, which is somewhere we know that they've been drinking at since they'd arrived. We spend an hour in there having a drink and planning our next move. All the time we're in there, the owner looks a bit on edge. He knows his bar stays in one piece all the time us and the Burnley boys don't meet. We are fed up and all decide to go back to the hotel to get changed and just go out enjoy the night, and if we bump into them, well, fine all well and good. As we get up to leave, a taxi pulls up outside. Four blokes get out and don't move as they are frozen to the spot. Seconds later two more taxis pull up and the occupants pay and step out onto the path, and then another two taxis pull up. It's them, and they've unwittingly walked straight into us. Lard Arse the boxer, is the first one to get a clump, and he leaves his mates and wobbles off up the road at a brisk pace. If he could have run I'm sure he would have but for him it was physically impossible, he was that unfit. Peg Leg, the birthday boy, has taken refuge under a table and as expected, isn't quite as brave as he was earlier on in the day. If I could have got my hands on a birthday cake, I'd have celebrated by squashing it into his ugly mug. We smashed them to pieces; they didn't stand a chance.

We fucked off before the coppers arrived and headed back to our hotel. Revenge is sweet and is a dish best served cold, so they say, but revenge served hot in the heat of a Bulgarian summer aint bad either. This time all of us have got away, unlike the first battle we had with Burnley when we had two nicked. Next morning over breakfast we sit around chatting about the previous day's events.

"Let's find their hotel and give them a visit," suggests one of the lads.

"Come on, it's our last day here so let's leave with a bang", and he meant it. When we were in Sofia he'd gone into a shop and bought some S.A.S. type thunder flashes and smoke grenades, which were perfectly, legal out here. You could buy almost anything over the counter in Bulgaria except that is decent food. One of our lads nips down into town and asks an English girl, who worked in one of the bars, if she knew where this Burnley firm were staying. She made a phone call to her mate in another bar who came up with the name of the hotel, which was not far from where we were staying. An hour later, we landed on them and it was like World War fucking three, a thunder flash is lit and thrown into the bar where they are sat drinking, followed by a smoke bomb. The hotel management and the guests must have thought it was a terrorist attack. As we cleared the place, as people went in all directions. Johnnie was again quick to hit the deck as his mates ran off and left him. Their super extra heavy weight boxer must have been in some serious training because there was a half-eaten extra large cheeseburger and chips left on the table where, only moments before, he'd been sitting. One of our lads wasn't quick enough in getting away and was arrested by the local Old Bill.

If you are ever thinking about going to Sunny Beach I wouldn't bother. There's nothing but trouble out there, and it's full of hooligans.
On the flight home, I was deep in thought my mind went back to when the Burnley mob had collared the six of us out shopping. I turned to "H" who was sitting next to me.
   "That Burnley Johnnie with the dodgy leg".
   "Who? Johnnie the carpet? " Smirked, H.
   "Johnnie the carpet?" I asked looking back at H blankly
   "Well, he was always on the floor", laughed "H".

Wolves started the season with a good 1-0 away win at Man. City. We then drew 1-1 with Pompey at home. In the July before the season kicked-off we lost the legendry Steve Bull with a serious knee injury the club were preparing for a pre-season tour out in Sweden when he broke down in training and after that he never played for wolves again, But what a bargain he turned out to be. The club reportedly paid £65,000 for him from West Brom and what a loyal servant he turned out to be at one time nearly every big club in Europe would have loved to have signed him, but he stayed loyal to the club something you very rarely hear of these days. The Tipton Terror as he was known to the fans once scored 52 goals in a season and while at Wovles won 13 full England caps. He scored a total, of 305 goals for Wolves in a career that spanned from 1986 to 1999. He finished his career at Hereford United where he played for a one time under the former Wolves manager Graham Turner. In the September, England beat Luxembourg 6-0 at Wembley in a European qualifier, and four days later draw 0-0 with Poland, in Warsaw. A few of the Wolves lads went out there and it goes off before the game in an arranged fight in a park in the city centre. Polish skinheads stab a few English boys and within hours, pictures of the row are on the Internet. For England to qualify for the Euro 2000 finals, Sweden would have to beat Poland, which they did, and England would then have to qualify via the play-offs, which was against the Jocks over two legs. The first game on the 13th November was to be played at Hampden.

On the night before the game about 60 of us lot from Wolverhampton booked into the Travel Lodge in Hamilton, which is just a short journey from Glasgow city centre. Half of us went off to East Kilbride to meet up with some lads from Plymouth and Huddersfield. The rest of the boys go out to sample the Hamilton night-life but it all ends with a mass brawl, with the locals taking exception to a mob of Englishmen in their town, drinking in their pubs and trying to chat up their women. One pub is completely wrecked and it only ends with the police arresting all of our lot. Some are released on the Saturday morning and a few are held until Monday morning. For the ones that still have their freedom, we catch an early train into Glasgow. When we arrive, there's Old Bill everywhere and mobs of English are spread out all over the place. Chelsea and West Ham are viewing one another with suspicion from opposite sides of the road, 70 Geordies are on the look out for a mob from Middlesborough and 40 Villa have just been caught and done by a big mob of Blues in Weatherspoons pub. Word on the street was that earlier that day, a tight mob of West Brom, had arrived early in the city centre and were, met by a Jock firm from Hibs. It kicked off and the Albion lads ran the Jocks everywhere. A couple of hours before kick off and this massive mob starts, to move off. The Old Bill was in front of us on horseback clearing a way through. A few Forest lads chase a mob of Jocks that come out of a pub, up a side street, but the Old Bill quickly round up the Forest lads and put them back in the escort. This England mob must have been 1,500 strong and it's all boys who look as though they're up for it. We have that many in numbers, the Old Bill are stretched to the limit. The police escort is all over the place and where gaps appear, the English slip out and have the odd scuffle with the Jocks who, as we pass where they're drinking, come out of the pub and square up to us. However, we're having none of it. We steam in at the first opportunity. I'm about halfway back in the mob, and up ahead the Old Bill is still trying to clear a way through. We're now spread across the road and are walking down both sides of the street. The traffic is at a standstill. People that are brave enough come out of their homes to look at this invading army. In other houses the curtains just twitch and move as they watch from inside.

The stadium comes into sight as the Jocks make a feeble attempt to come through the Old Bill at us. "Aberdeen", "Aberdeen", chant the Jocks, as the Old Bill push them back towards a pub which is stuck in-between a row of bleak, grey coloured, terraced houses. Across the other side of the road another fight breaks out, and the Old Bill leave the Jocks outside the pub and rush off to quell the new outbreak of violence. I rush towards the pub and crack one of the Jocks on the jaw, and he goes down like a sack of shit.

"Aint so mouthy now yam ya cunt" I shout at him, as he looks up at me from the floor. A hand grabs me firmly on the shoulder and pulls me away through the crowds.

"Gilly, watch yaself mate".

I've never seen this geezer in my life before.

"Who are you mate?" I ask.

"I'm a Blue", he replies.

"Be careful, the Old Bill are watching you", he says, looking all around and disappears into the crowds. Who the fuck was he? I didn't even know the bloke but he seemed to know me. He even knew me name. Strange that if he'd had a mask on I would have sworn it was the Lone Ranger.

Up at the ground the Old Bill throw a cordon of bodies around us and let out the ones amongst us with a valid match ticket. The rest are escorted back to the train station where we're split up into smaller groups. We're then allowed onto a train, which is stopping at Hamilton. Out of our Wolves lot there's only about 8 of us left, with me, Tyson and Carlton being the older ones. As we sit back on the train and look out of the window, standing there on the platform are a dozen Albion lads. We pull down the windows, as they looked shocked to see us.

"Come on lads, jump on" we shout. A copper strolls over and in a heavy, Glaswegian accent tells the Albion boys to, either get on board the train or face being nicked. The Old Bill start getting heavy-handed and try pushing the Albion lads on with us. It's not until one of them points out to the Old Bill who they are and then points at us and tells them, who we are, that the Old Bill start to listen, and the penny drops. The train pulls out, minus the lucky West Brom scum, oh what fun we could have had!

We arrive back at the digs in Hamilton, pack up our kit and head off to Blackpool for the night, and what a night we had, but that's a story for another time.

We never saw a kick of the game, which England won 2-0, with both goals coming from Paul Scholes. The return leg was four days later down in London, and I went with me mates, Faza and Chinney in his Mum's car. We parked up in central London and headed for where we thought all the English would be, but to our surprise, the Jocks were everywhere. Trafalgar Square was just full of them. We bumped into a little group of Plymouth that I knew and we were joined by a couple of Arsenal lads. As we chatted, a group of Jocks came bouncing over.

"Come on England, we're Partick if ya fancy it". They were a right bunch of scruffy cunts. They had nylon anoraks on, striped tank tops and green flash trainers. They looked the type to have a stray dog on a bit of string whilst selling the Big Issue. Anyway, Chinney cracks one of them and it goes off. Then a bloke who looks like the fella off of the porridge oats advert comes storming towards me and Faza, " come on yous English cunt" he screams in my face I look at Chinney and whack this geezer as hard as I can he goes over a wall which as a 10ft drop on the other side. They go mental and want to kill us, as the Old Bill lead us away. We were so disorganised and I never saw a proper England mob all day long. I ended up watching the game, which we lost 1-0 but still went through on aggregate, in the Sports Bar over near Holborn. I was surrounded by city types in their designer suits and shirts and ties, more interested in talking about who they wanted to shag in the office and how much money they earned, than paying attention to what was happening in the football.

Around about Christmas time, Wolves played Walsall away, which is a local derby. We knew we wouldn't get a row with Walsall because they don't really have a mob. After the game, which ended in a 1-1, draw about 70 of us jumped on a train, and got out at Birmingham New Street. The Blues had just been playing Stockport County at St. Andrews. We had no Old Bill with us and it was 6.30 p.m. so all the shops would be shut and all the shoppers long gone home and the streets deserted. As we come out of the station we headed for Bar St.

Martins where we know we'd find a mob of Birmingham. This was one of their favoured watering holes. A few of our lads went off towards the bar in the station.

"Get the fuck out of there" I shouted, "they won't be in there".

Before we could get to the doors of Bar St Martins, the bouncers standing out the front see us coming and rush inside and try to shut and lock the doors, but their boys inside, fair play to them, pull at the doors and force them open, the doormen are pushed to one side, and they pile out, throwing glasses and bottles at us. We back off a few yards as their ammo lands short of us. It was even numbers and I'd have to say we were just getting the upper hand when the Old Bill arrived and pushed us back into the station. We had no injuries and only one arrested, a bit of a result I'd say.

Not content with turning the Blues over, we went on a bit of a suicide mission and on the way back to Wolverhampton about 20 of us got off at West Brom and went into one of their pubs. They'd been playing at home that day but they soon heard we were in town and turned up outside, 50 handed, and it was all their boys. We came out and I hit one of them with a stool I've taken from the pub. Some of our lot bottled it that night and they melted away. I stood and fought and for a couple of minutes I was a bit of a punch bag. I took a right beating and some of the Albion boys saw that as a bit of a result. We only had half a dozen main lads with us. We had four girls and a lot of young lads with us so I can't see how they can claim a result. One of their big fat cunts put it about that we'd had a straightener and that he'd done me, one to one. Dream on Fatso. You didn't even land a punch. You were too busy eating your extra large donner and chips and licking the chilli sauce off, of your fingers

That season, on April the 1st, we played the Blues at St. Andrews. One of the boys booked a double Decker bus and we all crammed on there. We took the back roads from Wolverhampton into Birmingham, as we know the Old Bill wouldn't capture us because they were busy controlling a march by striking car workers. The Blues were on the phone on the journey down, which is only about 10 miles and half an hours drive. Anyway, we wouldn't tell them where we were heading and every five minutes they were on the phone.

"Where are yowl?" But we wouldn't let on what we had planned. We eventually stopped at the Breeze Bar, which was well out of the way but easy enough for them to come to if they fancied it. We phoned them back and told them where we were, and waited, and we didn't have to wait long. I was sitting outside drinking a can of Coke when I spotted a group of about fifty blokes moving towards us from the left, Two of our lads, who'd been out scouting and getting some grub came running back just as they appeared.

"They're here, they're here," they said, trying to catch their breath.

"Not to worry, I've seen them," I said, as I got to my feet and walked towards them. They'd arrived in taxis for the ten-minute journey to reach us, and fair play they'd made the effort and it was their top firm All their old Zulus were in the mob to our left and a bigger mob of about 80 come from the other end of the street, to our right. It seemed like this Birmingham mob were out for revenge after we landed on them after the Walsall game. We'd heard they wanted revenge badly and they were going to do this and do that and were even calling today the day of fools, so our lot empty out of the pub behind me and a flare is fired into them, that's followed by a petrol bomb which goes off and explodes which stops them in their tracks. We steam into both sides of them and the ones on the right start to back off and then have it on their toes. The older ones on the left keep coming forward, and are well game, but we don't give an inch and keep backing them up. A couple more flares are fired into them and orange smoke drifts across the street, bodies are lying motionless on the floor. Bricks and bottles have caused injuries on both sides, one of ours is hit with a brick over the head and ends up in a coma, in hospital. This row went on for a good 20 minutes before the Old Bill turned up and put a stop to it they chase the Birmingham lads that can move back up towards the city centre and round us lot up and escort us to the ground. After the game finishes, we storm the gates to get out at them and they have a massive mob trying to get at us. I reckon that fight, ended Birmingham's reputation as a top firm. Their bubble had been well burst and after that mad, mad mental day, they were never the same with a few of their lads even retiring from the scene. After that, many of their top boys drifted off into doing other things.

Some worked and ran the doors of local pubs and clubs, others got into the fag and booze runs from France, others, the snide, designer gear, and what did their top boy do? He appeared on Family Fortunes with the rest of his clan. He'd really hit the big time and found his true vocation in life and just to give you a clue, who he his, he has the same name as Michael Jackson's pet monkey. Got it?

Wolves at this time not only, I would say, had the best firm in the Midlands but we probably had the best mob in the whole of the country. On our day we were awesome and there wasn't a lot of mobs that could touch us. Another firm who tried it with us on around this time were Leicester City's Baby Squad. They'd been playing West Ham at Upton Park and we were away to QPR at Loftus Road. After the game our lot were drinking in the Flying Scotsman near Kings Cross, as usual I got bored and me and me mate, Bell, went off for a walk. Standing outside the Euston Flyer pub was a group of lads. I recognise one of their lot, Yeoman, from England games.

"Where's ya firm?" he asks cockily.

I pull my phone out of my pocket and call up the lads.

"I bring ya a firm" I tell him, and within seconds our lot come screaming around the corner. Yeoman is punched to the floor as we destroy them. They got fucking hammered as we attack the pub. They knew we were the top boys and they never crossed swords with us again. The same with West Broom, they kept on phoning us and calling it on after they thought they'd had that result against us when we done that suicide mission. Now they were getting a bit big for their boots. We played them but none of us went to the game at the Molineux, instead a 150 strong mob sat in a pub that was easy for them to get to and waited but their mob but they never turned up at the pub or down at the ground for the game. Two hours after the game, 17 of us went to a pub we knew they'd been drinking at earlier on in the day. Most of our lot had drifted away, fed up waiting for them after they promised us that they were going to show, but the ones out of us that were left went by bus over to them. The pub they were in was full as one of our lads kicked the doors open and hurled in a smoke bomb. They tried to get out but one of ours was waving a crowbar around and they couldn't get past him. One of them inside the pub must have phoned all the other pubs in the area because a mob of theirs came out of The Marksman, and out of The Hop Hole, they came from everywhere. There must have been 200 of them and they run us everywhere we were well out numbered. As we were being chased up the road, a rubbish skip came into sight.

"Stop at the skip and load up", somebody shouted.

We stopped, breathless and near on exhausted, at the side of the skip. Inside wasn't the usual things people throw in skips like builders' rubble, bricks, wood, metal piping, anything you could perhaps use as a weapon in a situation like this. No, inside this skip, was just old thread bare carpets. I suppose we could have given them a shake and held them at bay with the dust! We took off again with them in hot pursuit we all done a left at the next crossroads but Dime Bar, one of our lads, has chosen to go right and dive under a hedge row in someone's front garden. But has he's dived in the intruder lights have come on and showed up where he's hiding the Albion lads have caught him straight away and given him a right hiding. They go to town on him and drop a paving slab on his head. When we get back into Wolverhampton we do a roll call and discover that Dime Bar is missing. I phone him on his mobile to see where he is and if he is all right he answers his phone and it turns out he's in hospital being stitched up, but he's a tough fucker and it didn't take long for him to recover.

The next time we run into West Brom was at their last game of the season. They were away to Preston and we were on a day out to Blackpool. We were playing at home on the Sunday so we decided to go on a day trip knowing that a few of their lads would travel up for their game the night before, and as Preston aint a million miles from Blackpool we knew they would be about.

We get to Blackpool at around 11 a.m. and the very first pub we walk into we bumped straight into a few of them. It was their fancy dress day and a few of them were dressed as Batman and Robin, and Superman and Rambo. Anyway, they looked right pricks.

"Go and get the rest of ya boys and bring them back here" we told them. A few of our lot wanted to do this group of Albion but that would have only made us bullies, like them. We'd given them a squeeze so we would wait and see what happened. My fat mate appeared outside, the one who reckons he done me in a straightener. He was unaware we were in the pub so I tapped on the window. His face was a picture when he saw me and he was off like, he had a rocket up his arse. We waited in the pub for a few hours and then we heard they were in a pub just up the road. Me and me mate went up there and tormented the life out of them. They could take it no longer and roared out into the street. Our lot left the pub and we went straight at them. They were shit and went in every direction. That's the trouble with them. If they have a little result against us they'll gloat about it for ages, but when we batter them it chokes them to admit it. Take it from me, they're fucking shit and they've got the cheek to call us Dog Head Dingles. That's from a team that wear shirts made out of Tesco carrier bags.

Wolves finished 7th that season as Charlton went up as champions. Still, not to worry. Euro 2000 out in Holland and Belgium was about to start on June the 12th and so with Kevin Keegan now in charge, expectations were high.

CHAPTER ELEVEN

EURO 2000

The draw for the European Championships pitched England against old adversaries, Germany, Portugal and Romania, thirty of us set off from Wolverhampton in two mini-buses for the drive down to Dover where we picked up 4 Plymouth lads, we then go straight through Customs with no bother or checks and onto the boat for the sailing across to Calais.

We'd watched the first game against Portugal on a giant screen in a pub in Wolverhampton, and what a game that was. England went 1-0 up after only three minutes and then the perm-head Scouser, McManaman, adds a second on 19 minutes, and England are cruising. At that stage it looked like we were going to notch up a hatful, but before the cheers and celebrating had time to die down, Portugal's Luis Figa pulls a goal back, and what a silly, weak goal it was to give away. He was allowed to run a long way towards goal unchallenged before hitting a long range shot past David Seaman. Shortly before half-time Portugal equalised with a diving header from Pinto. The England players looked stunned as the pub fell silent. In the second half, Nuno Gomez struck after 60 minutes and it was game over as England huffed and puffed but never came near to scoring again. We trudged from the pub dejected, let down by another poor England performance. The team always seem to promise so much but never seem to deliver when it comes to the big games.

I promised myself I'd do my bit for revenge, not be throwing bottles at the coppers waiting outside the pub, but I would not drink Matteus Rose or eat Peri Peri chicken or sardines for a few weeks.

We arrived in Calais and were waved straight off the boat and straight through Customs. No checks, no questions, we couldn't believe it. The tabloids, along with the football Old Bill, had made such a song and dance about them watching and monitoring who attended the championships and that they would be stopping known troublemakers. Well there was no one to greet us. Perhaps we didn't fall into any of their categories. Perhaps the authorities didn't perceive us as troublemakers, or perhaps we had only kidded ourselves that we were the chaps. Frightening aint it?

After getting lost a few times on route, we finally rolled into Brussels. Even crossing from France into Belgium there were no border guards. We found somewhere to stay, dropped our kit off, got showered and went out to play. The first watering hole we came across was O'Reilly's Irish bar and it was jammed packed with English lads, and the booze was flowing. A few Blues were getting a bit boisterous with a few locals. Next thing words are exchanged and then it goes off, with bar stools and glasses and bottles flying through the air. We managed to get out before the Old Bill turned up and when they did, they took no prisoners. As I said before, these cunts don't fuck about. They are brutal bastards. They laid into people, beating them to a pulp. We nipped up the road a bit lively, and standing outside a sort of wine bar, we saw Tucker and Steff, and a few other Villa lads. We all went inside out of the way and got ourselves a drink. Next thing we know the doors have burst open and in walks this Belgian copper dressed in a rubber boiler suit with a breathing mask on and a big tank with a nozzle on it strapped to his back. He then squirts the whole place with C.S. gas, and fuck me was it strong. I've been sprayed with gas before but fucking hell, this was industrial strength. Every cunt inside was choking and even the bar staff copped it. When Robo-Cop the copper started squirting it about, the spray was that powerful it knocked the optics off the wall from behind the bar. The only thing to do was to get out and into the street. You had no option. Some crawled out on their hands and knees, they were that overcome. I was fucking choking to death and my face was burning and my eyes stinging and running with floods of tears. As I stepped outside and took a huge gulp of fresh air. I was grabbed and flung to the floor. I then had plastic handcuffs tied around my hands and wrists, which were then pulled up behind my back. I was in agony as my face was rammed into the pavement the skin on my face was burning like fuck. I just wanted to reach out and rub and scratch my face and eye- balls but I physically couldn't because I was trussed up like a Christmas turkey.

Recording all this was a film crew who were making a documentary. A few months later it was shown on British TV. Anis, a Welsh lad from Cardiff, who had been caught up in it all, was dragged from the bar and dumped on the floor he made out he was choking and couldn't catch his breath, the Old Bill released their grip on him and stood back to give him some space to get air. That was it, he took his chance and leapt to his feet and was off. "Mind you" as the Welsh say, he didn't get very far before he was pounced on and wrestled to the ground. This time the coppers take no chances and were almost sitting on him, to hold him down. Nazi Germany springs to mind on how we were being treated it was a fucking disgrace. We were told to sit still on the cold damp pavement we'd been dumped on and after a while we were allowed to stand up, but were told to say nothing as the cameras rolled. There was to be no talking to each other said the S.S. man in charge, "no talking". I could just about breathe, let alone fucking talk, what with all that gear they'd sprayed us with, it was a wonder no one was killed? The only light-hearted, funny moment to come out of it all was when the film was shown. You could see Abbo one of the Wolves lads, leaving the bar with a lighted cigarette hanging out of the corner of his mouth! How the fuck anyone could smoke a fag, with all that C.S. gas in the air I just don't know. It was like motorway fog and you could hardly see your hand in front of your face it was that thick.

We sat there for quite a time while the Old Bill showed off their captives to the assembled press. Cameras flashed as reporters, with mobile phones glued to their ears, shouted excitedly down the lines, no doubt telling their colleagues on the news desk just what had gone on or, more likely, what had not gone on. It was a fucking circus, I was expecting to have my head shaved and put into a striped prison uniform. One at a time we were led onto a coach and driven to what looked like a holding prison. The contents of our coach were frog marched into a large cell with rusty metal bars on the windows. It measured about 50ft x 50ft and had no furniture, just bare, grey walls and a grey cracked concrete floor. We were ordered to sit down and be quiet. Our handcuffs were released as the Belgium SS spaced us out.

"No talking," barked one of the officers. A few people asked if they could use the toilet. "No", came back the short sharp shouted reply. I was held like this for nearly 24 hours and in that time, all I was given was a clear see through plastic like surgical bag full of cold water which you had to squeeze to get a drink from, and to eat we were given one cold potato waffle. Some people on not being allowed to use a toilet were pissing themselves where they sat.

In the cell next door, which was the same size as ours and contained the same amount of people, they had it even worse. An argument broke out between them over-aggressive coppers and a couple of the England boys who rightly so, were getting pissed off at being kept like battery hens. If we had been badly treated animals kept in the same conditions the R.S.P.C.A. would have come and rescued us, voices were raised as fans demanded to be, either let go or be able to see someone from the British Embassy. What did the Belgiums do? They drove a water canon into the yard outside, pulled the high-pressure hose up to the door, and sprayed everyone with cold water. You should have heard the shouting and cursing. Now some people might say that it served us right as we'd gone looking for trouble and we'd found it, but we weren't causing any bother. Can you imagine the outcry if a group of Belgium football fans were rounded up in central London, locked up in a disused warehouse, not fed, and doused in ice cold water? I'll tell you, it wouldn't happen.

I was released after seeing a doctor. I complained of feeling unwell and was taken out and examined. I had to sign a form that said, in effect, that I would not attend any football matches whilst in Belgium. This I did and I was released immediately, a few others done the same thing, and got out.

I jumped into a cab and went back to my hotel. I hadn't slept for 24 hours, and looked and felt like shit. I took a shower, brushed my teeth and had a shave. I looked in the mirror and asked myself why I should listen to them Belgium no good mothers cunts. They can't tell me what to do. I got dressed and headed for the railway station, England, were playing the Germans in Charleroi, which was about 45 minutes on the train from Brussels. I bought a rail ticket and was looking up at the departures board when two very drunk Scotsmen approached me.

"Want a ticket for the game?" one of them slurred. We negotiated a price and I ended up buying two tickets off them for face value. I couldn't believe my luck and on the train on the way down I end up selling one to an English geezer for £80. At the other end I jump into a taxi to take me to the stadium. We pulled up and I paid him the fare. As I step out of the taxi I look around to get my bearings I realise we've stopped smack bang in the middle of a 250 strong mob of Germans, and they look like they can have a row. These are all big, strong German storm trooper types. The thing is I stand out like a sore thumb. I'm ya typical English football fan dressed in baseball cap, Lacoste polo shirt, cargo shorts and brilliant white trainers, and I've just landed smack bang in the middle of a firm of Germany's finest. Three of them come bouncing towards me, arms open wide in a pose favoured by most hooligans who are calling a row on.

"Where are you from?" one asks.

"Wolverhampton", I reply.

"Steve Bull, ya?"

"Fuck Steve Bull" I said.

The Old Bill had been watching this mob and come to my rescue by moving the Germans on. Fucking hell, that was close. The thing is that they weren't dressed and didn't look any different to how our boys dress. Quite a few of them had "Stone Island" tops on. It seemed the fashion the English have set and worn over the last few years at football, has now spread around the rest of Europe. It was not that long ago most fooball mobs in Germany, Holland, Poland, etc. were dressing as skinheads with cropped hair and nylon flight jackets and looked like members of the British National Party. How the times had changed.

I took up my seat in the tiny stadium and chatted to the blokes around me. The game had already kicked off and they told me there'd been a little skirmish between the English and the Germans in the bars around the main square. It had been a bit of a "handbags at ten paces" with the two mobs of shirts just throwing plastic tables and chairs at one another, before the police eventually broke it up with a water canon. A few of the English lads treated it as a joke and dived into the torrent of water as if it were a water ride at Alton Towers, they threw themselves into the powerful stream of water, arse or chest first, and allowed the flowing river to send them across the drenched square at high speed all good harmless fun by the sounds of it. Alan Shearer scored with a typical Shearer header in the 53rd minute to give us a 1-0 victory. Outside afterwards, the Old Bill kept rival fans apart and there was no real trouble to report.

The next day the F.A. was warned by U.E.F.A. that if the English fans misbehaved again then we would be expelled from the tournament. The next morning 4 of us left Brussels for the return journey home, 34 had made the trip out here but 30 had been deported, many being flown home on an R.A.F. Hercules, to Stanstead, and some to Manchester.

The last game of the group saw us lose 3-2 to Romania, which I watched at home on the telly. We needed just a point to go through to the next stage, and after leading at half time, the Romanians then equalised and then won the game with a penalty given away by Man. United's Phil Neville. The one consolation was although we didn't go through neither did the Germans, who finished bottom of the group with just one point.

Wolves started 2000-2001 with two 1-1 draws, at home to Sheffield Wednesday and away to Stockport. Next, was Burnley at home, which we won 1-0, and there was no sign of Jake the Peg and his crew. We thought they might turn up after their humiliation out in Bulgaria. We turned out in big numbers but they never showed. By the sounds of it, they only travel to near neighbours Blackburn Rovers who don't have a mob anyway, and its only 8 miles from Burnley, but they don't seem to travel very far to other games.

Next game up was Pompey away. A few of the boys travelled down for that one but nothing really happened, even though we lost 3-1. England's next game was against Germany at Wembley in the October in a World Cup qualifier. If I didn't know better I'd say this draw had been fixed, how many times have we been drawn against them in competitions, in the last few years? It seemed well hooky, but on paper, it looked like we had a good chance of getting to the finals out in Japan. In our group, along with the Germans, were Finland, Albania and Greece. For the start of the Germany match Kevin Keegan baffled many by playing Gareth Southgate in an unfamiliar midfield role, and it back-fired badly as we went down to a goal from Deider Hamann's long-range free kick, which skidded off the rain-sodden pitch and somehow under keeper Seaman and rested in the back of the net.

This was the last match played before Wembley was closed and pulled down, and the fans noisily let Keegan know just how they felt about this result. However, as the players disappointedly trudged away, soaked by the never-ending, evening rain, even they would have no idea what awaited them on the back pages of the following morning's tabloids.

Wolves meanwhile, saw Dave Jones, the ex-Stockport and Southampton manager, installed in place of the departed Colin Lee who'd had two seasons in charge and had taken the club only as high as a seventh place finish. This season under Jones, we went backwards and finished 12th. Not really, an improvement in anyone's book, but given time he would change the club's fortunes around. One could row we had around this time was with Doncaster Rovers, down in London. They'd been some-where like Wycombe, or Woking and we'd been playing someone else in the capital. There was about a 100 of us drinking in the "Flying Scotsman" when a small group of Arab looking geezers came in offering to sell us Coke and puff, we were just about to give them a dig and fuck them off out of it, when a mob of about 60 lads appear outside the pub it turns out these lads are Doncaster's main firm and call us outside for a row, we don't need asking twice and steam straight into them a couple stand and take a right battering but the rest we chase up the road and into a pub, the pub is then smashed to pieces with the Donny lads trapped inside its dark with no street lights in this road and a police car pulls up to see what's going on but they don't bother to get out to investigate instead they lock themselves in the patrol car. They were all big geezers and were well game but they were well out of their league by mixing it with us.

CHAPTER TWELVE

QUITTERS AND SHITTERS

To everyone's surprise Kevin Keegan quit the England job directly after the Germany game at Wembley. He said he'd taken the team as far as he could. Peter Taylor and Howard Wilkinson were put in temporary charge and in their first game, four days after Keegan's resignation; we drew 0-0 with Finland, in Helsinki. The next international game I went to was in June when we played against Greece in Athens in another World Cup qualifying game, and England had a new man in charge, Swede, Sven-Goran Eriksson, who had taken over the reins as head coach.

Me and 25 other lads from around Wolverhampton booked a week's holiday on the Greek Island of Zante, and the plans we had in mind was to catch the early morning ferry across to the Greek mainland, but at one stage it looked like I would be missing the trip. A few days into the holiday a load of us went off and hired motorbikes and scooters, and we were tearing around Zante like a gang of Hell's Angels. We'd roar through sleepy country villages and scare the life out of the locals. I had me mate, Millsey, riding pillion with me, and I started to get a bit cocky and confident and I was overtaking and braking in front of the others and forcing them to brake sharply. Just really fucking about and acting the clown, the next thing I know I'm skidding along the tarmac road on my arse with my legs trapped under the bike and Millsey travelling along on the deck next to me like we were a motorbike and side car team. We'd skidded on a patch of oil as the bike was whipped from under us. I got to my feet shakily and could just about stand as I was in fucking agony. I looked around at the others who'd pulled up straight away to see how we were. I knew by their faces they were trying not to laugh. A few of them were trying their hardest to stifle laughter and huge grins were being covered with their hands, the bastards! I had a quick look at my injuries, and I'd taken the skin off my ankle nearly down to my bone and it was stinging and throbbing like fuck. Millsey had a badly grazed leg and had ripped the flesh way from down near his shin, but at least we were in one piece.

The next morning when I tried to stand up, I was still in agony. A few of the lads suggested that I go to the hospital and have it x-rayed as they suspected I may have broken or fractured my foot and ankle, but I'm a stubborn cunt, and just to have some bubble doctor look at it would have cost me a fortune. That's the thing on foreign holidays, if you have to go to a clinic or a hospital they charge you a fortune. If you try and claim it back on your insurance (that's if you have any), they don't like paying out and I wasn't going to waste my money for a thirty second consultation and a £100 tube of cream. Fuck that.

On the day of the game I hobbled onto the boat at 6 am, with the rest of the lads, with the sea crossing and the coach journey at the other end, we finally arrived in the centre of Athens at around 2 pm, where we met up, with Nicky (Big Dick) Smith another Wolves fan who'd travelled to Athens from the holiday island of Rhodes. Nicky's party trick is that he can completely fill an empty pint glass with his dick and that's not with a hard-on, that's when it's soft. I don't want to sound like a shirt-lifter, but his knob is fucking huge. We were out in Wolverhampton one night when this old bird in her late fifties came over and asked if it were true that he had this massive tackle. She was a game old sort because she trusted Nicky to stick his throbbing Cory into her mouth as she sank to her knees. What she didn't tell him was that she was wearing false teeth and as he withdrew it, out came her teeth on the end of his helmet!

After an hour or so, the bar we were in began to fill up. A few Plymouth lads had a bit of an argument with a couple of the locals and one of the barmen, who made it his business to get involved. A small Sheffield United firm, eyed a mob of their rivals, Sheffield Wednesday, who were standing at the opposite side of the bar. It had been the same on the boat trip over. They'd just stared at one another. I couldn't see that happening if we were sharing a boat with West Brom. It would have been off before we'd left the port. I was surprised because for two firms that supposedly hate one another they certainly were well restrained towards each other. Anyway, the locals were back for round two and it goes off again. Glasses and bottles are thrown between the two sides. I pick up a round, wooden table and the top comes off in my hands. I throw it through the air like a plastic Frisbee and it hits a Greek geezer straight on the jaw and sparks him straight out. Tommy Smith, a Plymouth lad, who also has a talent like Nicky Big Dick, says to me

"Do you play darts for a living, Gil?" "Because if you don't you should do!" His talent involves being able to get his cock out and piss a huge jet of golden rain over his shoulder without getting soaked! It's a pity Hugie Green and "Opportunity Knocks " is no longer on the telly because I think Nicky and Tommy would have been neck and neck on the old clapometer.

The Greek Old Bill turn up and me, Tommy, and Nicky who has a slight gash on his head, fuck off a bit quick, well as fast as we could because I was hobbling along on one foot. The rest of the boys are rounded up and put onto a coach where they are held until just before the game is finished. They are then released with no charges. Before the game it goes off around the ground with the English and the Greeks. We pay at the turnstiles and go in. Inside the atmosphere is well hostile and flares and rockets are fired by the Greeks into the English section. After the game, which England won 2-0 with goals from Scholes and David Beckham, we were informed by the police that there were no more buses running to the port that night and the earliest bus would be the next morning at 7.00 a.m. Four of us then decided to find a taxi to take us back to the port, and as we look for an empty cab to flag down, we bump into "Bernard" and "Sweat", two of Albion's main boys. The last time we'd seen them was when we were out in Bulgaria and they were out there with their wives. I get on well with "Bernard" who's a good lad, but if some of our lads had seen him then they would have given him a squeeze. Something would have been said to the pair of them, as our lot wouldn't let them both get away Scot-free. We pay £60 to get back to the port only to be told the first ferry out to Zante leaves at 4.00 a.m. Spike, one of our lot, who is no taller than 5ft and has no teeth and is an alcoholic, gets the shakes and desperately needs a drink. On the quayside is a cupboard made of old rotten wood so we pull the half hanging door off and break in hoping we may find it full of booze and a quick fix for Spike, but all are disappointed when we find it's filled with bottles not of beer wine or spirits but with water.

On the domestic scene Wolves, under Dave Jones, start the 2001-2002 season with a 2-2 draw with Pompey. We then win 8 and draw 2 of our next games. Our first loss of that season is at home to Crewe.

The next England game I go to is out in Germany where I'm unknowingly filmed for that television programme the one, where they called me Lenny. I'd gone out to Germany with two mates in a car I'd borrowed off another mate who was on holiday in Majorca. We'd arrived at the Channel Tunnel crossing, in Nosha's Saab convertible and was then held for 45 minutes by the Old Bill and the customs, who just didn't believe that we were not off to Germany but were having a weekend away in Amsterdam. After a while, they let Lanney, Ben and me go because they could find no evidence that we were off to watch football in Germany.

When we got across to France, we decided to lower the soft top down and drive across Europe in style with the wind blowing in our hair. What we didn't know was that we'd broken the hood putting it in the down position and couldn't get it back up when it got a bit over-cast and nippy so we had to do the 20-hour trip down to Munich freezing our bollocks off. Serves us right for posing. We got to Munich and pulled up outside the main train station and look around for the rest of the lads. We're stopped by two English, plain clothes Old Bill who ask how the fuck we'd managed to get out there without being held on the English side of the Channel. They run a check on the car and ask us, which one of us is Harry Rock, which is Nosha's real name, and is part of the car's number plate.

"None of us" I reply, "He's sunning himself in Majorca".

They were fucking fuming and desperately would have loved to have nicked us but we'd not done anything wrong so they had to let us go. However, I just knew that one day they'd get to have the last laugh.

In the October, England were playing the home qualifying game against Greece at Old Trafford and 5 of us travelled up to Manchester for the game. Carl, Abbo's brother, knew a few Burnley lads so we teamed up with them and went looking for a watering hole, strange things happen in football especially after what had gone on with the Burnley firm and us out in Bulgaria I'd personally would have thought they would be the last mob we'd go out on the piss with, but there ya go!. As we walked up the street we passed another group of lads.

"Come on ya Manc cunts," said one of them.

"Fucking Mancs" said Abbo, "we're Wolves", and we got straight into them and done them before they struggled free and ran off up the road. From a pub across the street appears a mob of Tranmere and another group of Burnley who have been drinking together and have just witnessed what's gone on. One Tranmere geezer makes himself busy and starts acting the hard-man he finds out who we are and tells Abbo he's looking for me. " Where's Gilly? Where's Gilly? I want Gilly" he shouts at the top of his voice. Abbo does no more and points at me.

"You've found him mate".

He walks towards me, and I bang him with a peach of a punch and he's out cold before he hits the deck. I heard later that he was unconscious for a while and spent a couple of days in hospital. We fucked off and kept our heads down.

The next time England played up in Manchester we turned up there 80 handed, but none of the other firms came out to play.

England qualified for the World Cup finals after a late Beckham goal against the Greeks, gave us a 2-2 draw.

In the February of 2002 England had a friendly against Holland, out in Amsterdam, and a few of us went over by car. Again the little shit faced rat who done the undercover filming was out there. Again I had no idea at the time what he was up to. He told me he was a Villa fan but what he didn't show on his programme was me getting a bit of a hiding off a mob of Albion out in Amsterdam. A mixture of Albion and Blues were drinking in a pub, and had seen us go past with that they came out and came straight into us. I looked around as I was surrounded by them I chinned one and put him on his arse, and then realised there were only three of us that had stood. The rest of our lot, and there were some proper faces amongst us, had ran off. We were soon overrun and in the end I was left on my own. I was getting a bit of a kicking when one lad stopped it all.

"He's on his own and he's had enough" I heard him say, and it ended. I was disappointed with out lot and the ones that ran off were nick-named the A.A., which stood for the Amsterdam Athletes. Afterwards, rumours went around that I'd been beaten unconscious and thrown into the canal, which was total bollocks. I admit I got a good kicking but that's life; if you live by the sword then you die by the sword. The people who let me down know who they are, but it's all in the past. I think I learnt a valuable lesson that day and those that ran, if they're honest with themselves, would say that they learnt something about themselves as well.

Wolves finish the season in 3rd place, 3 points behind West Brom in 2nd and 13 points behind champions, Man. City. Birmingham finish 5th, 10 points behind us and a have a point more than 6th placed Norwich City, who beat us in the play-offs 3-1at Carrow Road, but lost at our place 1-0. They then play and lose to Birmingham in the play-off final. We really should have got automatic promotion that season but we stumbled at the last hurdle. The last 4 games saw us lose at Man. City 2-0 away and to Millwall 1-0. We then beat Wimbledon at home 1-0 and on the last day of the season, after being 2-0 up at Sheffield Wednesday, we throw away a two goal lead and drew 2-2 while the scum up the road won, and grabbed the other automatic promotion place. Still, worse things happen at sea.

In the May of that year, after my appearance on T.V., a few of the tabloids ran stories about me and on how I was supposedly planning a £3,000 trip to the World Cup out in Japan. One paper claimed that I was "the baddest in Britain" and that I'd been banned from matches for 11 of the past 14 years. Apparently, according to them, I'd been planning this trip to Japan for months and that I was boasting that "I'd been done more times for football hooliganism than anyone else in Britain". Funny that because I don't recall speaking to any newspaper or journalist about anything to do with football, the World Cup or anything else come to that. It was a totally fabricated story with not a hint of truth in it. I had no intention of travelling to Japan. For one thing I had no money, I was living at my Auntie's after splitting with Debbie, and any money I had saved was going to go on decorating and furnishing the house that me and my son, Adam, were about to move into.

Out in Japan, England drew with Sweden 1-1 in the first game and beat old rivals, Argentina, 1-0 with a Beckham penalty, in the second. In the last game of group F we draw 0-0 with Nigeria and finish 2nd in the group behind Sweden. In the second round knock out stage, we destroy Denmark 3-0 with goals from Owen, Ferdinand and Heskey. We then meet Brazil in the quarter finals where, after a promising start and a goal from Liverpool's Michael Owen, we then hit the self destruct button and allow the Brazilians to play their passing game, which they did, and duly scored two goals, one from a slick interchange of passing, and the other from a long-range, Ronaldino, floated free kick, which somehow went over David Seaman and into the net.

That was it, England were out and packed and on the plane back home, to some this was, yet again, another disappointing series of perform-ances in a major tournament. Some of the media even called for the England coach's head, but he was made of sterner stuff and vowed to carry on, and he proved that he was neither a quitter nor a shitter.

CHAPTER THIRTEEN

"THE PROMISED LAND"

After last season's disappointment of losing to Norwich City in the play-offs, a lot of people were expecting us to do better this season. We kicked off with a 0-0 draw against Bradford City followed by a defeat at Wimbledon 3-2, then we were back to Selhurst Park the following week where we lost 4-2 to Crystal Palace. We then lost at home 1-0 to Reading and things weren't looking too good. A lot of fans were calling for manager, Dave Jones's head, but the following week we thumped Preston 4-0 at home. Now we were up and running only to see us lose our next two games against Leicester and Sheffield United. We were piss poor but in the F.A. Cup we came into our own. We beat the Geordies 3-2 at home and then demolished close rivals Leicester, 4-1 at The Molineux. Then in a live T.V. Game, we done Rochdale 3-1 at our place and were then through to the quarterfinals where we were paired with Southampton, down at St. Mary's. It seemed we had more chance of getting to the F.A. Cup final than gaining promotion to the Premiership. Thousands of Wolves fans made the trip to the South Coast but that was only to be expected, being just one game away from a semi-final place.

Our mob met up in the Matt Le Tisser's Feet Pub, which is not far from the ground. I'm sure the pub was called that. Still, one of you anorak wearing statisticians who might be reading this will, I'm sure, put me straight if I have the name wrong. Just before kick-off, the pub emptied and we decided to go and have a look around. There must have been about 250 of us and it was all our top faces. We must have done two laps around the outside of the stadium and never saw a Southampton fan who remotely looked like he or she was up for a spot of fisty-cuffs. In the end the Old Bill who'd been monitoring our unofficial tour of St. Mary's, decided they'd seen enough and herded us into the stadium. Inside it was clear that Wolves had sold their allocation of tickets and were out-singing the home fans. This could turn out to be the classic David and Goliath game with the First Division minnows knocking out the Premiership giants. Southampton are hardly giants but they once turned Man. Utd. Over in a Wembley final a few years back, a game, which I watched on T.V. when I was a kid.

On the pitch Wolves fanatical and vocal support done absolutely nothing to lift the team and at 2-0 down and with five minutes to go, hundreds of us left the ground. As we reached the home fans' end a scuffle broke out, and about 60 of us chased a crowd of Saints boys back into the ground. The Old Bill baton-charged us out of the stadium where more of our boys on seeing what was happening ran across and joined in. It then went from fighting with their fans to fighting with the coppers. They came into us smashing their batons down onto people's heads and a couple of them minus their truncheons were wrestled to the floor before we backed them off. One of the coppers who had a lot to say for him-self wouldn't let it rest and done a lone charge back into us. A Wolves plain-clothes spotter jumped in and pulled him away. He was heard to say, "leave it mate, this lot will kill ya". He took his advice and left it. We then split into two firms with 'H' taking his lot one way and the lot I was with headed back to the pub we were in before kick-off. After ten minutes, the Old Bill turn up and chuck us out, because they said we were upsetting the natives by drinking in the pub. More scuffles broke out with the locals, and the Old Bill grabbed whoever was nearest to them and arrested them, which included me. Twelve of us are held and told we're being arrested on a Prevention Charge and are taken to the local nick. We're in the cells for three hours and then released. The rest of our lot had gathered outside the police station and were refusing to leave until we were released. Now that's what you call friends!

A week later 100 of us were back in Southampton and drinking around near the docks. We were playing at Pompey and had come down by coach we then jumped on a train from Southampton to Fratton Park. It was a bit of a fuck up really because when we arrived at Portsmouth the game had already kicked off and the streets were deserted. I'd just been doing an interview for the Terrace Legends book, which I was going to appear in, and we'd sort of not noticed the time. Plus when we left Southampton we'd got on the wrong train and ended up getting off at Havant and jumping into taxis to go down to the ground. Afterwards we all came out together and as we walked back, to the station, a mob of Pompey came out of a side road and three Old Bill held them back. If they had wanted to, they could have quite easily come across the road at us. They certainly talk the talk but don't walk the walk. Don't get me wrong, I have the utmost respect for them but their days are gone. Before the game they were on the phone to us every five minutes asking "where are you, are you coming?" But I was disappointed with them. A few of their boys had come unstuck up at our place on the first game in the previous season. One of them had his mobile phone nicked and a few got whacked, and one had his Stone Island jacket torn and the badge ripped off, so they were looking for revenge. Still, going up this season, as champions and getting into the Premiership would have made them all happy. Now we were out of the F.A. Cup all we had to concentrate on was promotion and getting into a play-off spot.

In our last 10 games, we lost only once and that was the 1-0 away defeat at Portsmouth. We finished 5th and played 4th placed Reading for a place in the play-off final at the Millennium Stadium, Cardiff. We beat them 2-1 at home and four days later, away, we beat them 1-0 with a goal from Alex Rae. Sheffield United was then our opponents in the final.

Around the time of this particular season I'd had a few run-ins with our Old Bill. We were playing Forest at home, and I was standing outside a pub with a few mates. I wasn't drunk as I was only drinking coke. The Old Bill turned up and wanted to close the pub but why, I don't know, as there'd been no trouble. The next thing I remember was getting smashed over the head with a police truncheon, which split my head wide open. There was blood everywhere as I was knocked to the floor and handcuffed. Indian Joey, who was with me, was also jumped on and as wrestled him to the floor, they smashed the glass he was holding into his temple. Fucking hell, there was blood pumping everywhere. There was that much blood coming from him which was covering the footpath and running into the kerb and into the road that they had to hold him over a drain while he was handcuffed. We were both taken to hospital to have our wounds treated and then we were released. I was covered in bruises where they'd punched and flogged me with their batons. It was all on video yet no charges were brought against anyone.

Not long after that I had yet another brush with the law. We were playing West Brom. And me, and a few friends were walking near the ring road away from the ground when the Old Bill appeared behind us. One of them pulls out his baton, and hits me over the head and splits my skull wide open again. I'm taken to hospital for more stitches and this time I put in a complaint to the police about the two assaults that I'd suffered. A few days later, they turn up at my house and arrested me for various things they claimed that I'd been up to. I was found not guilty in court but no action was ever taken against them for the two assaults.

On my birthday about 40 of us went out for a drink in town. We were in the Walkabout Pub when about eight off-duty coppers came in. They've seen us and smirked. With them was the one that had cracked me over the head the last time, so one of us went over and told them it was better for them that they left. The arrogant bastards just laughed. One of them put down his pint, and strolled over all cockily and stood in front of me.

"It hasn't got to be like this Gilroy," he said, sarcastically, staring me straight in the face.

"You've changed ya tune", I said, "you were calling me a fat wanker not so long ago". One of their lot then came over and pushed one of ours, and that was it. A fag was dogged out on one of their necks and it just went off. We went to town on them and smashed them to bits. The Old Bill arrived and I was arrested but a couple of the doormen spoke up for me and told how the off-duty coppers were out for trouble they had flashed their warrant cards on the door of the pub when they came in and seemed intent on looking for confrontation. They even offered to show the arresting officers footage from the pub's C.C.T.V. cameras. "These lads were already in here and were causing no problems", said the head doorman. "They've done nothing wrong, it was your colleagues that started it". The police Inspector who was trying to get to the bottom, of it all made me promise to cause no problems, anywhere that night and that if I agreed he would de-arrest me. I agreed and was let go. Afterwards most of the coppers involved in the incident were put on police probation and were warned of their future behaviour.

Sheffield United in the play-off final down in Cardiff was a day out most Wolves fans were not going to miss. We'd not been in the top flight for almost 18 years. For me, if we beat Sheffield and got into the Premiership then it would be a dream come true, and I knew that went for a lot of people. We'd played United at Bramhall Lane earlier that season and I organised two coach loads of us to travel to the game. We were pulled over by the Old Bill in Chesterfield, but were allowed on our way to the game after a little warning about our intended behaviour. After the game, there was the odd scuffle here and there but nothing too serious. The Old Bill wanted us away and out of Sheffield as quickly as possible and despite our protests and explanations that we were travelling back on the coach that we'd arrived on, they slung us on the train. When the train stopped at Burton, about 60 of us decided to get off. After a couple of drinks, we decide to get back on the train and go and have a look around Birmingham. We walk around and the streets are deserted. Someone suggests having a look around West Bromwich so we jump on the train and head North. Albion had been at home to Liverpool that day so we knew they'd still be around, and sure enough, they were. They came piling out of one of their usual haunts, the Billiard Hall, and we chased them back inside and smashed them to pieces. It looked like I'd miss the play-off final because, not expecting to get there, I'd gone and booked a holiday to Thailand. My big day was saved though when I paid another £150 to move the flight to the day after the game.

The day before the big game, about 80 of us travelled down to Weston-Super-Mare for a night out. We'd booked hotels and a few of us had our girlfriends and wives in tow. We found a pub and settled down for a good night. A few of the single lads had gone on a bit of a pub-crawl and had landed on 50 Sheffield United lads. They came back for us and we went back up to the pub with them. Sheffield were well fucked, as they couldn't get out at us, as the windows went in, those of them that did manage to get out got well hammered. Afterwards when the Old bill had it under control, a few of them spotted me across the road and shouted that "I was tut lad off tut telly!"

"Fuck off", I shouted back. "You bunch of fucking idiots".

At the game, which we won 3-0, there was no trouble before or after the game. The Cardiff Old Bill have it well sussed out. I bumped into Mac from Cardiff who runs many of the pub doors in the city, and we had a chat about both being in the Terrace Legends book and about a certain fire alarm. He's a proper gentleman and has my utmost respect. Although I loved the fact that at last we were back in the top flight and were going to be playing in the Premiership, week in week out, deep down I knew I wouldn't be watching them because I had this court case hanging over me. This was the one, which stemmed from the previous years appearance on the BBC. T.V. undercover documentary. The court hearing was set for the same day as we played Man Utd, up at Old Trafford, so I phoned the court and told them that I was sick and wouldn't be attending that day and instead went up to watch the game, which we lost 1-0. Wolves didn't get off to a very good start and life was going to be a lot, lot harder in the top flight. Just to survive you have to spend vast amounts of money on quality players. You can't do it on a shoestring budget if you want to stay up longer then one season. We lost our first three games, 5-1 away to Blackburn, 4-0 at home to Charlton, and then we had that 1-0 defeat to Man. Utd. After that we got our first point with a 0-0 draw with Pompey. A few days after that I had my long-awaited trial.

I was placed on a two-year banning order at Wolverhampton Magistrates' Court. They originally wanted to make it a five year ban, but after a bit of discussion both parties agreed to a two year ban, which prohibited me from attending any football match in the U.K., and also included following the English or Welsh international sides, both at home and abroad. Part of the order is that I must be no nearer than 3 miles to any ground where Wolves are playing, and that I am not allowed in the town centre of Wolverhampton 3 hours before a game and 4 hours after a game. If I break or breach any of these rulings then I can face arrest and serve a prison sentence of up to 6 months. I was the first person to receive a banning order by the West Midlands Police.

Also, something happened that season that put everything into perspective. It even overshadowed my ban from the game, which I love. Fingles, the legend, sadly died, and over two thousand people turned out for his funeral. The traffic around Darlaston came to a standstill as he was laid to rest. The big fella was a larger than life character who was loved by everyone that knew him. He loved his holidays in Thailand and he was a big influence in my life. Even to this day we still speak and laugh about his exploits. He is sadly missed by everyone at The Wolves.

So that was it. I was banned. I can't really speak about what went on in our season in the Premiership but my mate, Carl, who is one of the chaps and has been with me in more that a few scrapes, takes over the story.

The Premiership

So it was finally here. After 19 years in the lower leagues, we had finally made it to the Premier. A lot of our lads, me included, had not seen us play top-flight football or if we had, we were only kids and couldn't remember much, so we were looking forward to some big clubs with some big firms or so-called names.

Man United

Mighty Man U was supposed to be going to smash us all over, as the season before they had gone to West Brom and took the piss. We looked forward to this with anticipation. We made a few calls and asked them what pubs they were gaping to, but they wouldn't tell us, well not until it was too late. Gilly was scouting around looking for them. Wolves tried to attack their escort but the Old Bill chased them back. On this day Wolves had good numbers, 250 good lads. There was only a few scuffles, one on the North Bank, which was toe-to-toe, and one whilst the game was on, where 30 or so Man U lads were having it rough as a lot of our banned lads, and those who don't go in, were chasing them everywhere. In the end the Old Bill got them and took them to the station. When we reflected after the game, we knew no one was going to come to the Wolves and take the piss.

Liverpool

No one expected to get much trouble against Liverpool. How wrong could we be? We had three rows in this season.

The first was at our place on a Saturday. It rained so much that they called the game off. We were all in the boozer by the train station. I was in the doorway of the pub talking to some lads on the front, when I saw 30 lads coming down from the station. We exchanged words and then Wolves came out of the pub and chased them back up the hill onto the station bridge. The Old Bill was running up from the station behind them. We stood facing each other and one or two got slapped and one Scouser got his hat nicked. As I said, the game was called off. The game was re-scheduled for a night game. A few calls were made amongst the lads and the Scousers said they weren't coming. But just before the game a Wolves lad, who was by the ground, got a whack and had his cap nicked so no one knew if they had travelled or not. After the game about 25 Scousers were picking on little gangs of Wolves. To be honest they were just chasing them about. The Wolves firm were in the town and later on about 10 of us confronted 15 of them. The Old Bill had got the rest. One of them had a razor blade on his tongue so we went up a dark street on a hill and told them to come. This is what they had come for after all, but they declined and the Old Bill then chased us off.

When we played Liverpool away, we met at the train station and there were about 80 of us. We got the train and decided to get off at Runcorn. We had a few drinks and then we heard that the train lines were down. The Old Bill had landed on us as well so we got taxis into Liverpool. The banned lads went to Manchester, which left about 60 of us in Liverpool. We went into Weatherspoons for a drink and then one of their lads, who is friendly with one of our lads, told us they were drinking on London Road. We gave the Old Bill the slip through the back door and marched across the ring road. Liverpool came around the corner, throwing glasses and bottles, and our lot run at them. They run off and some of them run into the pub. A few slaps were given out and the Old Bill, who were really pissed off now, nicked a few of ours when they were walking to the ground. After the game about 40 of us walked down the road. There was no Old Bill anywhere. We went to a pub on the estate called The Willow and we phoned them and waited an hour or more, but nobody showed so we got on the bus to Liverpool. When we got to the station, a couple of Liverpool appeared. We told them that all they had done was fuck us about. Then the Old Bill got wise and got rid of us. So, that was the end of Liverpool.

Everton

When Everton had heard about us with Liverpool they decided to bring a good firm to Wolves. The Old Bill had got a lot of them on the train and put them straight in the ground. There was 3 Space Cruisers of lads by a pub near the ground, who were bullying some young lads. Then a call was made and some of the older lads landed in taxis, which equalled the numbers. Our lads gave it them and they ran off. The Space Cruisers ended up being a draughty ride home. After the game there was a fight on the North Bank and there was a lot of trouble all across town, which was unexpected. Later on an Everton lad phoned us and told us it was fucking great and one of the best days they have had for years. They hoped we stayed up.

Middlesborough

Borough away was to be a sad day. One of our close lads and top boys sadly passed away. So we had a wake. We took a double Decker, a single coach and a few cars. We decided to dump them in North Allerton and get the train into Borough. We got off at the station and the Old Bill were there waiting. Borough came under the arch bridge and we went at them. The Old Bill beat us back and flogged us to the ground. We went in the match and came out a few minutes from the end. We decided to go left, and the next thing you know Borough came calling it on. Wolves just ran at them with the "who who" chant. Borough ran and this really angered the Old Bill who beat us back into the ground with the batons out. In fact they beat us all the way back to the train station. It was the first time ever that I made the 17:10 train. The Borough lads said we took a good mob and it was fair play for showing up. We aim to please.

A mention for the writer of this book – Gilly, who came, but had to stay 3 miles away. He was gutted.

When we played Borough at home we phoned some of their lads who said they were coming, but they parked their coaches in Cannock, which emptied. Borough didn't fancy it and turned their backs on having the row. They were game earlier when they had the numbers.

Birmingham

The Blues or 'No-Shows' have definitely lost it. Not much happened till after the game and it was much publicised in the local press and on television. The Blues fronted and got run. The ones that stood got hammered and the Old Bill filmed it. A few of the lads got banned but over all we were very disappointed with Birmingham.

Tottenham

The mighty Yids. Some of the lads spoke to them on the phone and they said they would be here at 11 o'clock "in ya boozer, we will smash ya". "Yeah, Yeah", I thought. We got the news they were drinking in Tipton in a pub called Mad O'Rourke's. Then when they came into Wolves with their escort, Wolves were on the 3 corners in 3 pubs, The Hogs Head, The Varsity and The Royal London. News came to us that they were on the ring road so we marched down the road. There may have been about 250 to 300 lads, one of the best mobs I've ever seen at Wolves. They saw us and we saw them. After the game there was slabs and bricks thrown at the Old Bill and the main mob of Wolves had been chased across a big car park. As I looked across, I saw a row going off on the middle of the ring road. 15 onto 15, it was proper. We ran back and could see that it was their main faces. One was crawling across the floor and one or two had bloody noses. The police dog was let off its lead and jumped onto somebody's back. A couple of Wolves lads got nicked and a few calls were made. We didn't disappoint and showed once again. We could mix it with the best and they said that they hoped to draw us in the F.A. Cup.

And finally a message to all of those firms or teams that we didn't travel to. After 19 years out of the top, everybody wanted to go to the games.

We knew that we would probably only have one season in there but we couldn't get the tickets. When you've been in the Premiership a few years the novelty wears off, so tickets are more available and everyone can travel. Still, there's always next time.

R.I.P. Premiership

After our short stay in the Premiership, here's just a couple of the highlights which happened the following season.

I couldn't write a chapter of this book without a mention of Cardiff. What a day! Gilly went to meet them and phoned us back. "If you aint got 150 forget it". This angered a lot of people as we had more. We out-stayed our welcome waiting for them to meet, and they never came. The Old Bill found us and escorted Wolves to their own ground. There had been some trouble by the ground before the game, 10s and 20s fighting, but that was nothing compared to what was going to happen after the game. 200 Wolves ran down the Cardiff end and threw crash barriers down on City. The Old Bill had to break it up and keep the fans apart. Police were attacked and 7 people had serious dog bites. There was fighting on the coach park and in the town centre, and one of the police dogs was stabbed. In the town after the game, Wolves had the best mob I have ever seen. There was 500 or maybe more. That day some of the local, shit fans (who for those that don't know are West Brom) were in the bus stop watching, and one of them reckoned the Wolves looked awesome. The Cardiff boys said "yam a top mob you am Wolves".

West Ham in the Cup

They had arranged to meet Wolves out of town, a few miles out, but never showed. Everyone was pissed off about that. It was a non-event before the game, but it was going off around the town after the game. Some West Ham lads got done in the town centre. The rumour was that one of them got stabbed with his own blade. Two were stabbed in total and one injured. All three were taken to the hospital. It was in the local paper that West Ham had taken a bit of stick that day.

Aston Villa

Aston Villa had arranged to meet out of town at a local tram stop but for some reason they got off 2 stops before and went into a snooker club in Bradley. When Wolves went up the road they didn't fancy it, and locked the doors. The Old Bill saved them. We know some of the Villa and they said they were disgusted when they locked the doors. The Old Bill chased the Wolves and we went back into town. The Villa faces were shipped back to B'ham.

Millwall. At home. Wolves turned a big mob out for Millwall after what happened in the night game a few years before with two of ours being stabbed. So it was game on. Before the game, Millwall turned up on the train and then went in an escort, to the game. After the game, Wolves tried to get at them but the riot police intervened. There was a lot of police pelted with everything, and then a little gang of Millwall and Wolves had a good toe-to-toe. Nobody won and then the Old Bill came and broke it up. Any Millwall lad worth his salt, even in the game a few years before when they used their tools, know that our boys didn't budge. You don't get 2 stabbed by running do you? And that night they clapped us. Fair play to them, they came on a Wednesday night and brought a good mob, and no one expected that.

CHAPTER FOURTEEN

FINAL THOUGHTS

As Carl said in his bit, we're now back in the First Division, which has now been re-named, The Championship. We've also seen the departure of Dave Jones as Manager, and Glen Hoddle has been brought in as his replacement. Euro 2004 has been and gone, and with it, the life of a Wolves Fan who was out in Portugal enjoying an evening meal when he was robbed. He gave chase to the man, a Ukrainian immigrant, who'd stolen his wallet, but was fatally stabbed as he apprehended him. I personally didn't know the lad but a few of our boys knew him and said he was a nice kid. I would have loved to have been out there and I really did have the urge to go, but with no passport, I had to be content with watching the games on the telly. Well, I do have me own passport but the police in Wolverhampton share it with me! Four days before an England International, home or away, I have to hand it in at the police station and I'm allowed it back one hour after the kick-off. About 50 of our lads made the trip out to Portugal but the only trouble was with the Portuguese Old Bill, and not with any other fans. A lot of them said the stabbing of the Wolves lad from Bushbury was hushed up and hardly made the news. Imagine if it was the other way round and English fans had robbed and stabbed a supporter from somewhere else. There would have been an almighty outcry and I bet the rest of Europe would have asked for our expulsion from the tournament. I can just see the headlines.

One of our lads, Boner, has just received a 5 year banning order where he has to be inside his own house one hour before a Wolves game and still inside one hour after the match has finished. He's also banned from the City Centre 4 hours before a game and 6 hours afterwards. He too has to hand his passport in for International games. I've now been banned from football for the last 13 years and I think when my current ban finishes, another I'm sure, will be put in its place. The Old Bill will think of something but I'm hoping I will keep out of trouble and get out to watch England in Germany for the 2006 World Cup. A leopard can change its spots, and I will prove it if allowed to do so.

A lot has been said over the last few years about the decline of the football hooligan, and the police through the media every now and then, release a statement to say that they are winning the battle in the fight against hooliganism. With more banning orders, more police and stewards, and C.C.T.V., they claim that the football hooligan will soon be eradicated. That may well be in the big, mega-bucks world of the Premiership, but down in the lower leagues, believe me, nothing's changed. You look at the unfashionable, so-called smaller clubs like Shrewsbury, Hereford, Aldershot, Newport County, Hull, Luton and Wrexham, who can all, on their day, pull a mob that would put their Premiership cousins in the shade. They're still doing it week in, week out, and it mostly goes unreported. Look at the likes of Cardiff who for years have had a top, top firm. I saw them first-hand a few years ago when they played a mid-week Cup game against Spurs. They had an awesome firm. Likewise so did the Yids who, at one point I swear, must have had a 700 strong mob out on the street. Love them or hate them, there's no denying that both clubs can pull a top firm when needs be, and by saying that I'm not sucking up to anyone. I was with me mates, young Carl, and Ginger Jason from Cardiff for that game, and it was going off big time before and after the game, and I'd give it honours even, you couldn't split the two mobs. Cardiff came up to our place recently and turned out in huge numbers. It had been billed as an England v Wales thing and afterwards it went mental, with the Old Bill struggling to keep the warring fans apart. But fair play, they turned up and came looking for it. Now adays the Old Bill have really got it sussed, but then again they're entitled to with the amount of manpower they deploy at a game and the amount of undercover operations and money they spend on intelligence. Just how much money do they spend? The way I look at it is the fighting's between two groups who want to fight, so why spend obscene amounts of taxpayers' money on preventing it?

Some might say football fans should be more adult and behave at games and then there'd be no need for a large police presence at football matches. Point taken, but I've ever only fought like-minded people.

We had a P.C. Clive Whitfield as our football intelligence officer and he was a proper gentleman. He has since retired but we used to have a right laugh with him. One Christmas we sent him chocolates and pink, fluffy handcuffs from all us boys. He had a great sense of humour. If he was waiting outside a pub for us and was watching what we were up to, we'd send him out packets of crisps and bottles of pop and he loved it. He was only doing his job but he done it with a smile on his face. I had the utmost respect for him and I often see him around town and stop and say hello to him and have a chat. I've bumped into him when he's been out having a meal with his wife and I've been with my girlfriend, and we've introduced our other halves to each other. His mum lives down near me and she's the same, a lovely old girl. As I say, I've got total respect for him, unlike the bloke that took his job. He's the complete opposite to Clive.

Looking back, I don't really have any regrets about the things I've done in my life. I look at it as some things I've done wrong and some I've done right, and as you get older you tend to get wiser and start to do things a little bit different from how you would have done things a few years ago, when younger. I don't smoke and don't drink and I don't take drugs, and I preach to my children the dangers of alcohol, ciga-rettes and drugs and I just hope they listen to me.

Recently it was my birthday and so, when Wolves were playing down in London against Millwall, about 40 of us came down by train for a day out in London. You know, have a few drinks, have something to eat and generally let our baldheads down. Well, none of us have any hair left! Another 50 came down by coach and to be honest most of them were intent on going to the game. Anyway, at some stage or another the plan was that we'd all meet up. Well, that was the plan but as soon as the coach reached the outskirts of London, it was pulled over by the Old Bill. Everyone on board was searched, names and addresses taken and then fucked off out of London. Seven of us travelled across London from Marleybone to Waterloo Station. Just outside the station, we counted 17 police vans with policemen many dressed in full riot gear, looking as if they were about to go into action. We thought there had been some sort of security alert and that was why the police were there in numbers. That was until we saw four Wolverhampton coppers pointing us out to their colleagues from the Met. We were quickly surrounded and stopped from moving. Passers-by must have thought we were terrorists or something. Talk about an over-reaction. The Wolverhampton Old Bill pointed out to me that my banning order prevented me from going within 3 miles of a football ground where Wolves were playing. The Met Old Bill and the Wolves coppers walked away out of hear shot of us and went into a huddle and kept their voices to a whisper as I guess they spoke about what they were going to do with us. After a few moments the scrum of policemen untangled itself.

"Right you lads, we've worked out that you are, in fact, 3 _ miles from the New Den which means that although you haven't broken any law, we are going to arrest you on a prevention of the breach of the peace".

"You're having a laugh", I replied.

"Do I look as though I'm laughing Mr. Shaw?"

With that, they marched us off, and threw us in the back of a police wagon and produced a document that they asked us to sign. It was, in fact, a declaration that in effect said that if we were found back in South London in the next 24 hours then we would be liable to arrest. We all signed and the van pulled away. Half an hour later, we were dropped off outside Marleybone train station. As we stepped from the back of the van the copper driving advised us to get on the first train back to Birmingham, which we did.

Since I've been banned I watch lots of different games on the T.V. I love football and will watch almost anything. Conference league, Scottish, Italian, Dutch, Spanish, German, any game on telly I'll sit and watch it. According to some experts, there's no link between a real football fan and someone that enjoys a punch up at football. Do me a favour! Most people that enjoy a ruck at football also follow and love their team with a passion. You can follow your team, be a true supporter, and still fight for your teams' name and reputation surely? However, by fighting or taking your support to another level, is that being a hooligan?

Then you come to the books and the films about football hooligans. Some of the books are great and others are pure fantasy. I think most of us that have had something to do with the scene can spot a fake. The ones that write a couple of books and then set themselves up as experts make me not laugh, but cringe. I hear them on the radio waffling on about how they know how to put a stop to it. Don't make me laugh! These geezers have never thrown a punch at football in their sad lives. Just because you slip a Stone Island jumper on over your beer belly, that doesn't make you a football hooligan. Neither does having a shaved head. Then there's the ones that are invincible and their firms have never been done or run. Every mob's been done or run at sometime or another. I'd like to see West Brom do a book. Well, it wouldn't be so much a book; it would probably be a pamphlet. No, I'm being too generous, they'd probably only have enough material to fill out the back of a postage stamp.

I thought a few years ago that the bubble was about to burst with all the Hoolie books that flooded onto the market. Nearly every High Street bookshop stocks them so there must be a demand for them, and I think a book, if it's good, reflects the firm it's about. Cass and his I.C.F. books are not bad reads and the I.C.F. were undoubtedly a top in their day firm. What else can you say about them? The Soul Crew book is another great read and Cardiff are a top firm. You knew, guaranteed, they'd turn up. They'd never let you down. Pompey would always turn up in numbers but over the last few years aint the force they once were. Maybe their Old Bill as got a lot to do with that. However, Rob Silvester's book, the "657" is a book with quite a few untruths in it. At the other end of the scale, Jasper's book, Naughty, which is all about his days of following Stoke is an honest account and if you've read this and his book properly you'll know that me and the rest of the Wolves lads have had some real scrapes with Stoke over the years.

As I write my book, a Man Utd book has just come on the shelves and by all accounts it's a first class read, but then again United are another firm that's been doing it for years. Love 'em or hate 'em, nine times out of ten you find their firm, or they'll find you. They never disappoint and the same goes for Boro. Home or away on their day, they've got a good bunch of lads. Last, but by no means least, you have Chelsea who, in the 70s and 80s, would turn up at Wolves in their thousands. Between Kingy, Ickey and Chubby they have produced some really good reads.

In this book I've been honest in what, and how, I saw things. Some people might disagree with some things I've written, but it was the way I saw things. It was my angle, my view, how I interpreted events, how I saw things happen and unfold in front of my own eyes. If you think I've got some things wrong then that's your view and opinion, all I'll say is you weren't standing in my shoes supporting my team, be it with Wolves or England. The same with my T.V. appearance. The shit I got off certain people about that. I feel sorry for anyone who is set up like, I was set up, all that bollocks on telly proved nothing. The same with the Jason Mariner and Nightmare undercover expose documentary. It was trial by T.V. and the people involved and who were set up had no right to reply. It's total bullshit. Do the British public really want to watch crap programmes like that? Part of the evidence against me was that on the programme it showed me being searched. Whoa wee, big deal! Does that make me a bad person, because I'm being searched by a policeman? And that it's on film? How much money was wasted on both those documentaries and just what did they prove or tell the viewer? I was hung, drawn and quartered on national T.V. and because I didn't have the resources to fight back, I was thrown to the wolves, no pun intended! But it was even worse for J and Andy. They got prison sentences for trial by T.V. and where was the British Justice system the rest of the World supposedly looks up to? Since Jason's release from prison we've become good friends, and I wish him all the luck with the book he's written about his trial and his time in prison. Now let's hope the truth comes out and we find out just who the real villains are.

Some of these documentaries don't have a grain of truth in them and you'd learn more from something like the Football Factory film, which I really enjoyed. I love Frank Harper's part and he reminded me so much of our very own Howey, even down to the white mac and the check shirts. They're dead ringers for one another.

Well, I suppose that's it. I think I've covered just about everything. I'm now enjoying life with my son, Adam, and we're not only father and son but we're also best mates. He's even been out to Thailand on holiday with me and he's met all the Chelsea and Arsenal lads in the Dog's Bollocks bar. The time I went without him though I ended up with malaria, and in hospital with the suspected S.A.R.S. virus. It took me a good 3 months to fully recover from malaria but I have, and I hope to see you all out in Germany for the 2006 World Cup finals, God and the Old Bill willing, that is.

Cheers, and Best Wishes,

Gilly Shaw.

My final thoughts...

Football violence has finished, it's gone, the Old Bill has done their job, and the good old days have long gone. Them days of waking up on a Saturday morning buzzing with excitement for the fun, which lay ahead. When you could go to an away game looking for a good old punch up and if you where unlucky all you would come back with was a section 5 charge and the most you would get for that in court was a £50 fine, now your on a police video before, during and after a game. You can be pulled up and interrogated by the Gestapo. A prisoner of war would have more rights then a football fan plus you can now, get banned for minimum of 3 years, for really doing next to nothing. What sort of bollocks is that? Therefore, for me now it's all memories, a thing of the past. Anyway just a few points to clear up, as I finish writing this book. I've just read Cass Pennants new book *Top Boys* and quite interesting it was too, especially Mr. Koca Cola's part when he and his not so mighty 60 scruffs done 11 wolves and 5 Plymouth and I stood on my own against them, and yes, I got done, so fucking what, would anybody fancy there chances with the numbers of sixty onto one, but Mr. Koca Cola you didn't actually tell the whole truth did you now? Firstly nobody knocked me to the ground, Secondly, I never asked for anybodies help, and, thirdly I and lots of other lads have the video to prove it, as it was all part of the evidence when the West midlands police served a civil ban on me... oh and by the way Mr. Kola of the mighty Sandwell town, your on the actual video, and surprise, surprise your doing fuck all [top boy my arse] ha ha, plus a few other things to put right about the rumours and lies that you and your junkie mates have spread about the Wolves firm, like us lot beating up women and kids, well you can think and say what you like, but all the lads I've ever been with to football have never ever seen that ever happen before for example Steve Cowans, in his crap book, says the same thing about us, and doesn't tell the truth, they came out the ground at wolves a few years ago, 80 handed and we were waiting outside and chased them back inside, they where the ones, fighting and pushing each other to get back in the ground and it was them that was pushing and trampling on women and children to get away. Same as that prick that wrote the book about Portsmouth, and slagged us off, another fucking has been...